WEIRD DETECTIVE™

DETECTIVE
SEBASTIAN
GREENE

Script by
FRED VAN LENTE

Art by
GUIU VILANOVA

Colors by
MAURÍCIO WALLACE
JOSAN GONZALEZ (CHAPTER 1)

Letters by
NATE PIEKOS OF BLAMBOT®

Cover by
FRANCESCO FRANCAVILLA

President and Publisher **MIKE RICHARDSON**
Editor **SPENCER CUSHING**
Assistant Editor **KEVIN BURKHALTER**
Collection Designer **BRENNAN THOME**
Digital Art Technician **CHRISTIANNE GOUDREAU**

WEIRD DETECTIVE

This volume collects the Dark Horse comic book series *Weird Detective* #1–#5, originally published June–October 2016.

Published by Dark Horse Books
A division of Dark Horse Comics, Inc.
10956 SE Main Street
Milwaukie, OR 97222

DarkHorse.com

International Licensing: 503-905-2377
To find a comics shop in your area, call the Comic Shop Locator Service toll-free at 1-888-266-4226.

Library of Congress Cataloging-in-Publication Data

Names: Van Lente, Fred, author. | Vilanova, Guiu, artist. | Wallace, Mauricio, colorist, artist. | Piekos, Nate, letterer.
Title: Weird detective / script, Fred Van Lente ; art, Guiu Vilanova ; colors, Mauricio Wallace ; lettering, Nate Piekos of Blambot ; cover art, Guiu Vilanova and Mauricio Wallace.
Description: First edition. | Milwaukie, OR : Dark Horse Books, 2017. | "This volume collects the Dark Horse comic book series Weird Detective #1-#6 originally published June through October, 2016"--T.p. verso.
Identifiers: LCCN 2016041253 | ISBN 9781506700380 (paperback)
Subjects: LCSH: Comic books, strips, etc. | BISAC: COMICS & GRAPHIC NOVELS / Science Fiction. | COMICS & GRAPHIC NOVELS / Horror. | COMICS & GRAPHIC NOVELS / Crime & Mystery.
Classification: LCC PN6728.W439 V36 2017 | DDC 741.5/973--dc23
LC record available at https://lccn.loc.gov/2016041253

First edition: February 2017
ISBN 978-1-50670-038-0

10 9 8 7 6 5 4 3 2 1
Printed in China

DETECTIVE
SEBASTIAN
GREENE

The most merciful thing in the world, I think…

…is the ability of the mind to correlate all its contents.

For example, the retina, a literal **extension** of your brain, transforms **photons** of light into neuronal signals.

OHMIGOD
WHATTHE HECKIS
DO YOU SEE THAT

LOOKS LIKE A
A
A, UH

AAAAHH
Various organs in the ear canal transform **vibrations of air** into spatiotemporal patterns firing along a specialized nerve.

Raised buds on your tongue…
…G-protein receptors on the tiny hairs inside your nose…
POLICE LINE DO NOT CROSS
GOOD MORNING, FELLOW LAW OFFICERS.
THE VICTIM IS INSIDE?
…are but a subset of **touch,** sense receptors that cover skin, bones, muscles, blood vessels, **et cetera,** transmitting data on temperature, pressure, pain.
HE FOR ***REAL?***
DON'T MIND GREENE.
HE'S FROM CANADA.
GREENE!
DOWN HERE!
So you really only have **three** senses.
But **flatter** yourself into thinking you have **five.**
THIS ONE'S MESSED UP.
EVEN BY YOUR STANDARDS.

IT'S LIKE WHEN MY LITTLE NIECE EMPTIES A JUICE BOX.
SHE SUCKS IT DRY.
UNTIL IT IMPLODES.

STILL TRYING TO FIGURE OUT HOW SHE GOT IN HERE...
...WITH NO ONE NOTICING BEFORE THE POOL OPENED.
SO THIN SHE COULD HAVE SLIPPED IN THROUGH THE INTAKE VALVES FROM *THAT* WATER SYSTEM.
YES. THAT APPEARS TO BE THE LIKELIEST SCENARIO.
SHE COULD'VE GOTTEN, *UH, "SKINNED,"* ANYWHERE IN FOUR BOROUGHS, DUMPED DOWN A STORM DRAIN, AND SUCKED IN HERE...
NOW WE JUST GOTTA FIND HER INSIDES.
I'LL CHECK THE LOCAL BUTCHER SHOPS.
I GOT THE CHINESE RESTAURANTS...
SO EVERY OTHER DIVISION DUMPS IT ON *MINOR CRIMES* SO IT DOESN'T RUIN THEIR *CLEARANCE RATE.*
GREENE, TIME TO WORK YOUR *MAGIC.* YOU'RE PRIMARYING THIS MESS.
I LOOK FORWARD TO WORKING WITH YOU ON IT. ALL THE CAPTAIN HAS SAID ABOUT YOU--
DO I KNOW YOU, DETECTIVE...?
OH. *UH*-- NO ONE TOLD YOU?
SANA FAYEZ...
I'M YOUR NEW PARTNER.
NO, YOU'RE NOT.
GREENE...

NO, SHE'S NOT.
...SORRY YOU HAD TO FIND OUT THIS WAY, SEBASTIAN. THIS COMES STRAIGHT FROM ONE POLICE PLAZA.
I don't mean to sound condescending.
About your three senses, I mean.
NO MORE LONE WOLFING, BY ANYBODY...
But I have seventeen.
Rennakesh, for example, is the sense of emotionalocation.
You may sometimes get the feeling that the person you're with is "somewhere else" or "lost in thought."
PART OF THE NEW DEAL THE BOSSES MADE WITH THE UNION.
That's because dissonance between physical and mental locations causes fluctuations in the wave-length of your ultraviolet aura.
Actually, most Terran primates have evolved an ultraviolet-sensitive sensory organ.
You just need to be able to inhabit the ultraviolet spectrum in order to register it.
PURE "BUDDY SYSTEM" FROM HERE ON OUT.
By pinging my UV rays off of hers, I can reconstruct in my mind the space she currently inhabits in her own.

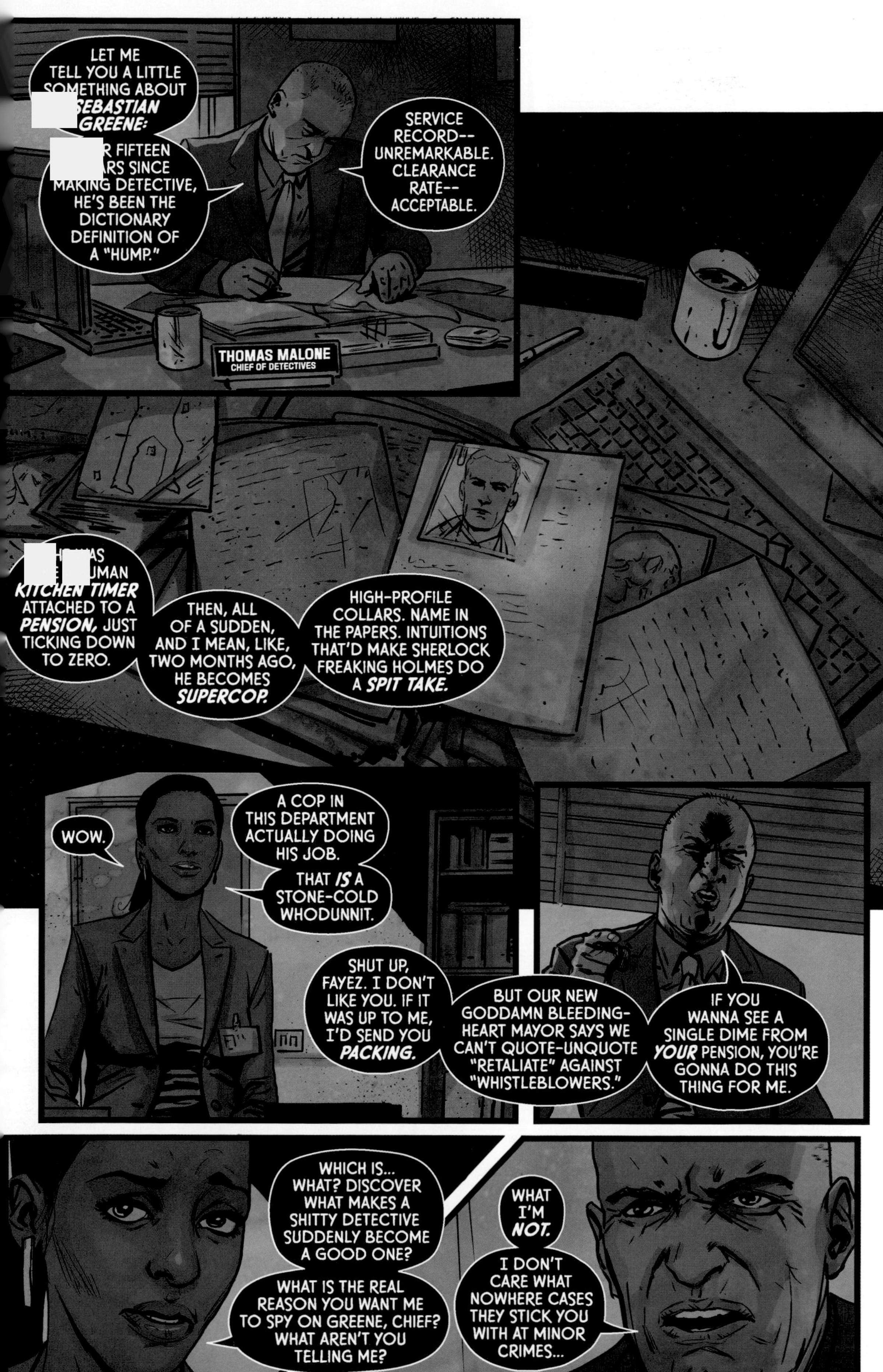
LET ME TELL YOU A LITTLE SOMETHING ABOUT SEBASTIAN GREENE:
R FIFTEEN ARS SINCE MAKING DETECTIVE, HE'S BEEN THE DICTIONARY DEFINITION OF A "HUMP."
SERVICE RECORD--UNREMARKABLE. CLEARANCE RATE--ACCEPTABLE.
THOMAS MALONE
CHIEF OF DETECTIVES
HE WAS UMAN KITCHEN TIMER ATTACHED TO A PENSION, JUST TICKING DOWN TO ZERO.
THEN, ALL OF A SUDDEN, AND I MEAN, LIKE, TWO MONTHS AGO, HE BECOMES SUPERCOP.
HIGH-PROFILE COLLARS. NAME IN THE PAPERS. INTUITIONS THAT'D MAKE SHERLOCK FREAKING HOLMES DO A SPIT TAKE.
WOW.
A COP IN THIS DEPARTMENT ACTUALLY DOING HIS JOB.
THAT IS A STONE-COLD WHODUNNIT.
SHUT UP, FAYEZ. I DON'T LIKE YOU. IF IT WAS UP TO ME, I'D SEND YOU PACKING.
BUT OUR NEW GODDAMN BLEEDING-HEART MAYOR SAYS WE CAN'T QUOTE-UNQUOTE "RETALIATE" AGAINST "WHISTLEBLOWERS."
IF YOU WANNA SEE A SINGLE DIME FROM YOUR PENSION, YOU'RE GONNA DO THIS THING FOR ME.
WHICH IS... WHAT? DISCOVER WHAT MAKES A SHITTY DETECTIVE SUDDENLY BECOME A GOOD ONE?
WHAT IS THE REAL REASON YOU WANT ME TO SPY ON GREENE, CHIEF? WHAT AREN'T YOU TELLING ME?
WHAT I'M NOT.
I DON'T CARE WHAT NOWHERE CASES THEY STICK YOU WITH AT MINOR CRIMES...

...YOUR *REAL* MYSTERY IS *SEBASTIAN GREENE.*

I DON'T SEE WHY THEY CALL THIS UNIT "MINOR" CRIMES.

A TEN-SPEEDER WITH HER EPIDERMIS PEELED OFF SEEMS PRETTY GODDAMN *MAJOR* TO ME.
OUGHTA CALL US *"WEIRD CRIMES."*
TO THE BRASS WE'RE "INCONVENIENT CRIMES."

SINCE MAKING GRADE I'VE SPENT MOST OF MY TIME IN COUNTERTERRORISM, DETECTIVE GREENE, BUT I'M A QUICK STUDY...
DETECTIVE GREENE?

THE DETECTIVE... HAS SOME *UNIQUE* METHODS, FAYEZ. YOU'RE ABOUT TO FIND OUT HOW UNIQUE.
WONDERFUL.

WHAT TIME YOU GET TO WORK?
EIGHT THIRTY, EIGHT THIRTY-FIVE...
FIRST ONE HERE?
YEAH, NOBODY ELSE COMES IN UNTIL JUST BEFORE NINE.
POOL OPENS THEN?
WHEN SCHOOL'S OUT, YEAH. BUT THEN FOR FALL HOURS--
YOU CLEAN THE POOL BEFORE OPENING?
YEAH, JUST SOME LEAVES, AN ACTION FIGURE STUCK IN THE--
WHY THE CAMERA?
DETECTIVE GREENE, IT'S ONE THING IF YOU WON'T PARTICIPATE IN THE INTERVIEW, BUT IF YOU COULD REFRAIN FROM...
...
WHAT'D YOU SAY?
THERE IS A HIDDEN CAMERA IN THE BOYS' SHOWERS AND LOCKER ROOM.
WHY IS THAT?

DAMMIT!
GREENE!
CIRCLE AROUND THE OTHER WAY! CUT HIM OFF!
ALL RIGHT.
Ranos, as the name implies, is the sense of reverse sonar.
Sonar uses sound waves to form the image of objects in front of you…
…this uses vibrations from the chest cavity to pass through the spaces between molecules...
...and form images of objects on the other side of obstacles.
And, vibrating at the right frequency…

NNAHH!
WAKK
HA!
YOU'RE UNDER ARREST FOR MAKING ME RUN IN THESE SHOES!
HOW'S THAT, MR. I-DON'T-NEED-A-PARTNER?
HUH?

SELLS VIDEO FEED FROM THE CHANGING ROOMS TO "KID FANCIER" WEBSITES.
LIKE THIS DAY COULD GET ANY GROSSER.
GET THIS PIECE OF WORK ON THE FERRY TO RIKERS BEFORE ANY OF THE LOCAL PARENTS TRY TO PEEL HIS SKIN OFF.
PART OF THE ENTREPRENEURIAL SPIRIT THAT MAKES THIS COUNTRY GREAT...
...BUT GIVES CREEPY JANITORS A BAD NAME.
GREAT WORK, GREENE--
--I HOPE YOU NEVER GET TIRED OF HEARING THAT, DETECTIVE, BECAUSE I NEVER GET TIRED OF SAYING IT.
IT'S JUST THE JOB, SIR.
DANG.
CAPTAIN LEONG'S TRYING TO FIT YOU FOR A HALO.
OR GET DOWN YOUR PANTS.
OR BOTH.
I DON'T KNOW WHAT YOU MEAN.
YOU DON'T THINK...
THERE'S NO CONNECTION BETWEEN PEEPING TOMÁS AND LITTLE MISS SKIN SUIT, IS THERE?
DEFINITELY NOT.
AS THE CAPTAIN SAID, THE VICTIM WAS NOT KILLED ANYWHERE NEAR THE POOL.
RIGHT. YOU WANT TO GO GET A BITE TO EAT? INDULGE IN SOME GETTING-TO-KNOW-YOU CHITCHAT?
I'LL START. I WAS BORN OVER THERE. ON ATLANTIC AVENUE--
NOT HUNGRY.
UH-HUH.
ANYONE EVER TELL YOU YOU'RE DEEPLY WEIRD, GREENE?

LIKE HE WON'T FIND A MARK ON HER.

...

REWARD

DIET FIZZO
YO.
POSEUR.

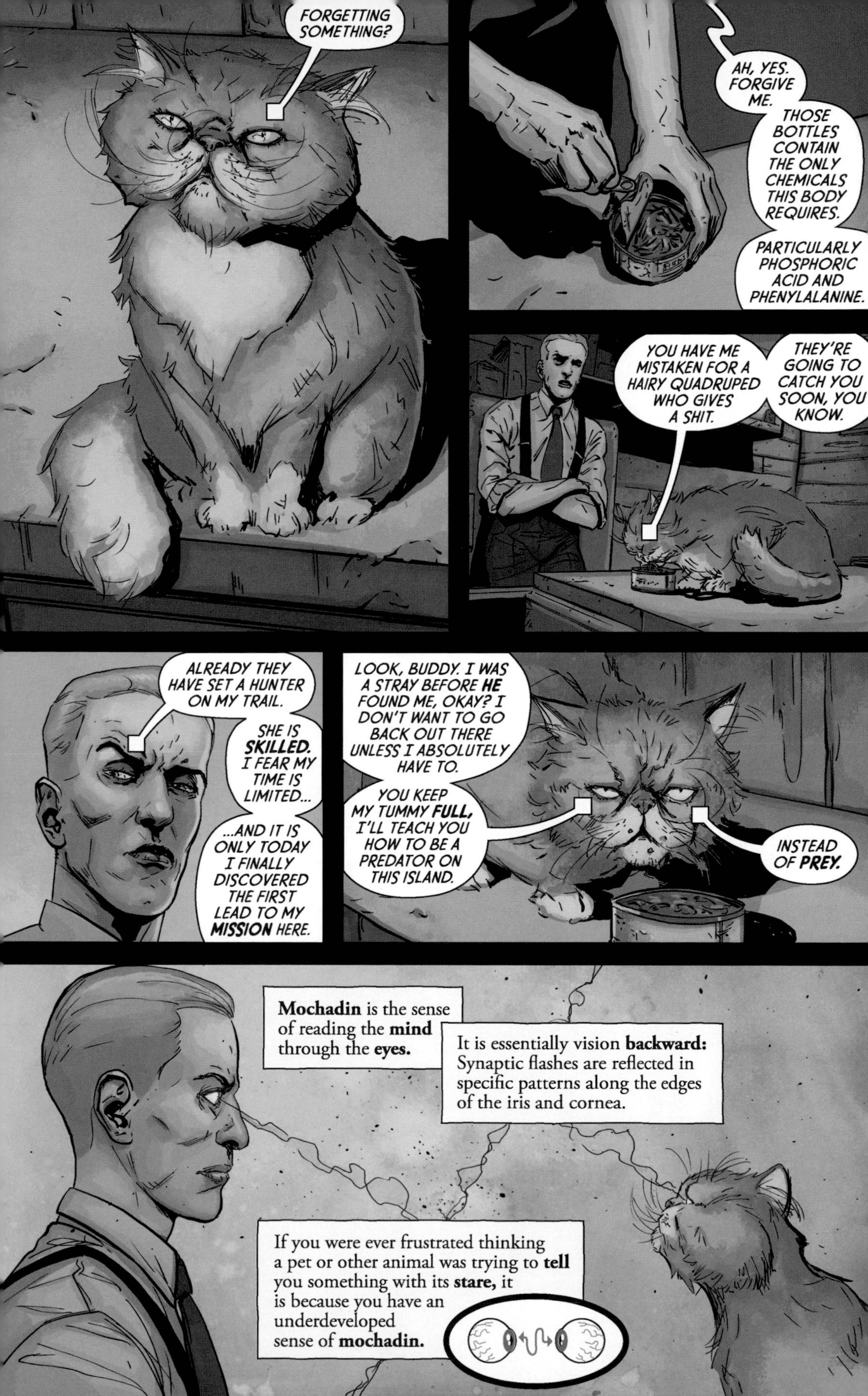
FORGETTING SOMETHING?
AH, YES. FORGIVE ME.
THOSE BOTTLES CONTAIN THE ONLY CHEMICALS THIS BODY REQUIRES.
PARTICULARLY PHOSPHORIC ACID AND PHENYLALANINE.
YOU HAVE ME MISTAKEN FOR A HAIRY QUADRUPED WHO GIVES A SHIT.
THEY'RE GOING TO CATCH YOU SOON, YOU KNOW.
ALREADY THEY HAVE SET A HUNTER ON MY TRAIL.
SHE IS **SKILLED.** I FEAR MY TIME IS LIMITED...
...AND IT IS ONLY TODAY I FINALLY DISCOVERED THE FIRST LEAD TO MY **MISSION** HERE.
LOOK, BUDDY. I WAS A STRAY BEFORE **HE** FOUND ME, OKAY? I DON'T WANT TO GO BACK OUT THERE UNLESS I ABSOLUTELY HAVE TO.
YOU KEEP MY TUMMY **FULL,** I'LL TEACH YOU HOW TO BE A PREDATOR ON THIS ISLAND.
INSTEAD OF **PREY.**
Mochadin is the sense of reading the **mind** through the **eyes.**
It is essentially vision **backward:** Synaptic flashes are reflected in specific patterns along the edges of the iris and cornea.
If you were ever frustrated thinking a pet or other animal was trying to **tell** you something with its **stare,** it is because you have an underdeveloped sense of **mochadin.**

IS MY...
IS MY SUBTERFUGE REALLY THAT POOR?
WANT A YES MAN? GET A DOG.
I'M GONNA TELL IT LIKE IT IS.
AND I CAN'T BELIEVE THEY HAVEN'T BUSTED YOU ALREADY.
YOU MAY SCRATCH BEHIND MY EARS NOW.
THANK YOU. FOR EVERYTHING...
...
WHAT IS YOUR NAME?
PRRRRR
NAME?
FUCK SHOULD I KNOW?
LIKE I GOT ANY USE FOR THAT SHIT.

OHHH... IT'S SO NICE...
YOU CAN'T EVEN TELL THERE'S ANY FLOOD DAMAGE...
YEAH, MY DAD IS REAL PROUD OF THIS ONE...

...SO TRY NOT TO TOUCH ANYTHING, OKAY?
ISLAND RENOVATIONS
OPEN HOUSE 7/1

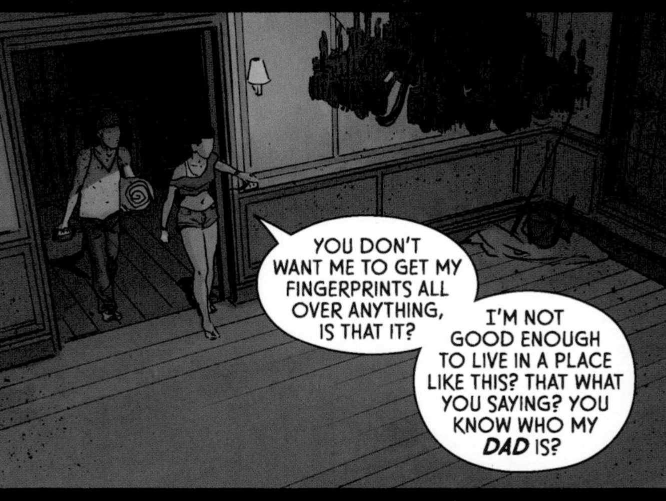
YOU DON'T WANT ME TO GET MY FINGERPRINTS ALL OVER ANYTHING, IS THAT IT?
I'M NOT GOOD ENOUGH TO LIVE IN A PLACE LIKE THIS? THAT WHAT YOU SAYING? YOU KNOW WHO MY DAD IS?

RAINA, I'M GONNA GET YOU THREE PLACES LIKE THIS.
ONE HERE, ONE IN L.A., ONE OVERLOOKING THE BEACH IN CABO...
YOU JUST FULL OF PROMISES, AREN'T YOU?

YOU INSPIRE ME TO MAKE OATHS.
OKAY, OKAY! QUIT IT! I'M STARVING.

LET'S EAT FIRST.
'KAY. GLAD WE TURNED ON THE PLUMBING IN THIS PLACE TODAY...
GOTTA LAY ME SOME CABLE...
DIDN'T NEED TO KNOW THAT!

HAVE YOU EV-ER THOUGHT A-BOUT
WHAT PRO-TECTS OUR HEAAAARTS
...
FOR SERIOUS?
YOU GONNA HAVE TO DO BETTER THAN THAT.
I GOT THREE BROTHERS. THREE ANZIO BROTHERS.
THEY KNOW HOW TO DO SOME SCARES.
THEY'D LAUGH YOU INTO THE STREET FOR...

PFFF.

DUMBASS...

KRRKK
POP SCKUK
KRRK
SPLK

GGKKLLKK
EEYAAHHH!
AAAHHH--

KLONG

WHUD

MY MIND REBELS AGAINST STAGNATION, WATSON. GIVE ME PROBLEMS... GIVE ME **WORK!** THEN I CAN DISPENSE WITH **ARTIFICIAL** STIMULANTS.
I CRAVE MENTAL EXULTATION. THAT IS WHY I HAVE CHOSEN MY OWN PROFESSION. OR RATHER, **CREATED** IT, FOR I AM THE ONLY ONE IN THE WORLD.

FOR I AM THE ONLY ONE IN THE WORLD...

I'M JUST A PRIVATE DICK ON A CASE.
Your **collective consciousness** is woefully **primitive.**

I AM JUST A DICK.
I AM JUST A DICK ON A CASE.

I HAVEN'T DONE ANYTHING WRONG, YOU CAN'T HOLD ME, SO BOOK ME OR LET ME GO!

I AM VERY CHARMING.
YOU WILL DO WHAT I SAY AGAINST YOUR BETTER JUDGMENT.

TURNS OUT SHE'S A **GRAD STUDENT.**
YEAH? SHE'S GONNA BE A COUPLE OF CREDITS **SHY.**

...A COUPLE OF CREDITS **SHY.**
HEH.
(MORBIDLY APPROPRIATE **QUIP.**)
Fortunately, the pursuers of **outliers** are among your greatest **cultural heroes...**

...and the contents of your technology-dependent **thought stream** help me maintain my **cunning disguise** in pursuit of my **mission.**
BRRR-BRRRR
THIS IS SEBASTIAN GREENE.
IT'S LEONG. DID I WAKE YOU?
NO, THIS BODY REQUIRES DEEP-REM SLEEP ONLY EVERY TEN DAY CYCLES.
WELL, GREAT, BECAUSE YOU CAUGHT ANOTHER BODY.
SAME NEIGHBORHOOD AS THE POOL, IN RED HOOK. SOME GIRL GOT TOSSED FROM A HALF-REFURBISHED BROWNSTONE.
MIGHT BE CONNECTED TO OUR OTHER THING. DOWNTOWN WANTS US TO CHECK IT OUT.
I SHALL DEPLOY IMMEDIATELY, CAPTAIN. END TRANSMISSION. CLICK
CANADIANS ARE WEIRD.
Months without a single lead. Now **two** in one day. Both auspicious...
...and **unsettling.** Time constricts until the stars are right and the horrors I have been sent here to stop awake and lead to the destruction of **my** world.
Sebastian Greene's body will serve me well in this regard...

...I hope he appreciates the experience of inhabiting mine.
AHHHHHH-- HELP ME!
MY NAME IS SEBASTIAN GREENE--
--I'M WITH THE N.Y.P.D.!
WON'T SOMEBODY HELP ME?!

NWAAAAAAA
WAAAAAAAA
I'M SORRY! GREENE AND I CAUGHT ANOTHER ONE! THE SQUAD IS SHORT STAFFED WITH THAT FLU GOING AROUND--
WELL, I'M BETWEEN TWELVE-HOUR SHIFTS!
I BARELY GOT ANY SLEEP AS IT IS, WITH HIM WAKING UP AT FOUR A.M.--
AND I HAVE A JOB WHERE I AM ELBOW DEEP IN PEOPLE'S GUTS ALL DAY!
YOU DON'T WANT TO PAY FOR A NANNY--
HE'S TOO YOUNG TO HAVE STRANGERS PAWING ALL OVER HIM--
THEN YOU HAVE TO TAKE HIM! THAT'S THAT!
BEV--
REMEMBER YOUR WHOLE "BEING DEMOTED FROM COUNTERTERRORISM IS A ***BLESSING IN DISGUISE***" SPEECH?
YOUR WHOLE "I CAN SPEND MORE TIME WITH YOU AND THE BABY" SPEECH?
WELL, YEAH, BUT THOSE WERE JUST ***WORDS.***
I DIDN'T EXPECT TO ACTUALLY ***DO ANYTHING*** ABOUT THEM.

AAAAAAA
AAAAAAAAA

NOT PROFESSIONAL, FAYEZ.
NOT PROFESSIONAL AT ALL.
SORRY, SIR.
AAAAAA
WON'T HAPPEN AGAIN, SIR.

AAAAAAAA--

WHOA. HE'S NEVER CLAMMED UP *THAT* QUICKLY BEFORE.

WILL YOU COME LIVE WITH ME?
NO.
I HAVE A CAT.

THAT WAS A JO...
NEVER MIND.
ISLAND

WHAT IS THE SITUATION?
LOOKS LIKE RAINA ANZIO'S BOYFRIEND CHUCKED HER FROM THE THIRD STORY OF THIS BROWNSTONE AND TOOK OFF FOR PARTS UNKNOWN.
SO WE'RE IN FOR A WORLD OF SHIT.
I MEAN, DO YOU KNOW WHO SHE *IS?*
YES. SHE IS THE VICTIM.
LOOK AT THE UNNATURAL WAY HER NECK IS TURNED.
I KNOW SHE'S THE...I MEAN, SHE'S AN *ANZIO.*
HER FATHER AND HIS BROTHER HAVE BEEN *KING GOOMBAHS* IN THIS TOWN SINCE THE LAST GOOD SEASON OF *THE SOPRANOS.*
WHICH WAS WHAT, *FOUR?*
THEY'RE NOT THE TYPES TO, YOU KNOW, STAY OUT OF THE WAY OF THE DULY APPOINTED LAW-ENFORCEMENT AUTHORITIES.
AND LUCKY US, WE CAUGHT IT. THE ONLY GOOD NEWS IS THIS SEEMS LIKE YOUR STANDARD CRIME OF PASSION--

WITNESSES SAY THEY SAW HER ENTER THE BUILDING WITH HER BOYFRIEND, EDGARDO NUÑEZ. IT'S EMPTY. THEY WERE GONNA HAVE SOME SORT OF INDOOR PICNIC...
Though your science has yet to discover it, you leave psychic impressions on the ozone in the atmosphere wherever you may be, residue as common as flaking skin scales or fingerprints.
The more intense these impressions, the longer they last--unless a storm front or low-pressure system comes through and wipes them away.
HE SWIPED THE KEYS TO THE EMPTY APARTMENT FROM HIS DAD, WHO'S RENOVATING THIS PLACE, POST-HURRICANE STEVIE.
NEIGHBORS HEARD SHOUTS, SCREAMS, AND BOOM--SHE'S DEAD, HE'S VANISHED.
The sense of **aushure** lets me read them.
They let me see:
The boy is innocent.
This is clearly also the work of the perpetrator at the swimming pool.
Good for me.
Less for him.
SHE WASN'T PUSHED.

WOW. THE TOILET TOLD YOU THAT?
HOW DO YOU KNOW, GREENE?
The captain never questioned my methods as long as I delivered the expected results.
Clearly this is no longer an option.
Not while my every move is being scrutinized.
A HUNCH.
A HUNCH! OOOOH! A HUNCH! YOU FIND ANYTHING ELSE OF USE INSIDE YOUR BIG BAG OF COP CLICHÉS?!
GGGII
NO.
ALL RIGHT, THEN, LET'S LET C.S.U. DO THEIR THING WHILE WE GET GUM ON OUR SHOES KNOCKING ON THE USUAL DOORS, HUH?
WE BETTER FIND NUÑEZ BEFORE THE ANZIOS DO.

Mine, if you will forgive me…
…is a **Great Race.**
Eons ago did we leave our dying world in psychic form to learn all we could from the depth and breadth of space and time.
Still. We went **together.**
All fears, hopes, dreams, loves, and hates, shared in a multifaceted stream of unified consciousness.
Now here I am, cut off from them, and I can barely handle the loneliness.
I close my eyes, and all I feel are the vastness and coldness of naked void.
You cannot fathom this.
Your mind reels from the possibility of its own insignificance.
I see evidence of this everywhere.
Mosque
GO HOME!
Your obsession with your own individual uniqueness.
Whether in the hatred of the **other…**
…or the fascination with the **self.**
You have no idea of the intimacy **I** have felt.

To you, the true love, bottomless, unconditional, of the Great Race…
…this is **horror.**

While to me…
…you are nothing but **monsters.**

DUDE.
DON'T ***STARE.***

HM?
DON'T... JUST, YOU DON'T NEED TO ***DENY*** IT, JUST DON'T ***DO*** IT.

AND I'M TELLING YOU, IF YOU HAVE ANY WEIRD, LIKE, PRINCESS JASMINE, BELLY-DANCING, *THOUSAND AND ONE NIGHTS* FANTASIES GOING THROUGH YOUR HEAD, KICK THAT SHIT TO THE CURB, OR I ***WILL*** DO IT FOR YOU.
I DON'T, *UH...*
AND HERE I WAS HOPING YOU AND I PLAYED FOR THE SAME TEAM.

I HAVE BEEN INVITED TO JOIN DEPARTMENTAL ***SOFTBALL TEAM,*** BUT FIRST I NEED TO ACQUIRE THE REQUISITE ***EQUIPMENT--***
NO, I MEAN I THOUGHT MAYBE YOU WERE GAY.

WE DO NOT HAVE THE "GAY" IN CANADA.
HA! JESUS, YOU ARE REPRESSED.
WHAT'S NEXT? YOU'RE GOING TO SAY THEY DON'T HAVE HOCKEY?
WHAT IS "HAKI"
ISLAND RENOVATIONS
HOPEFULLY EDGARDO SENIOR PLAYS IT SMART AND DOESN'T TRY TO COVER FOR HIS...
...SON...
AW, CRAP.

HOW DOES THAT GO, NUÑEZ?
"THE SINS OF THE FATHER... SHOULD NOT BE VISITED ON THE SONS."
OR DAUGHTERS. I DID MY BEST TO KEEP MY GIRLS AWAY FROM THIS GANGSTER SHIT.
MEN ARE EXPECTED TO BE WARRIORS. BUT RAINA... I DIDN'T WANT THAT FOR HER. SHE GOT OTHER RESPONSIBILITIES, OTHER DUTIES.
BUT YOUR SON... HE ENDED ALL THAT.
PLEASE...MY BOY WOULDN'T DO THAT...HE'S THE MOST GENTLE...THE KINDEST...
HE LOVED THAT GIRL...
I MEAN, ALL THAT SIN VISITING...I GUESS THAT WORKS IN REVERSE TOO, HUH?
IF IT WAS UP TO ME, FATHERS SHOULDN'T HAVE TO PAY FOR WHAT SONS HAVE DONE.
KREEEK
BUT IT'S NOT JUST UP TO ME.

MOTHERS GET THEIR SAY TOO.
AND SHE REALLY WANTS SOMEONE TO PAY FOR WHAT HE DID TO OUR LITTLE GIRL.

BRRR
BRRR
BRR
ANSWER IT.
YOUNG NUÑEZ'S CELL PHONE? WHY ME?
BRRR
BRRR
BRR
THEY'RE SURE AS SHIT NOT GONNA BELIEVE *I'M* HIM. DO IT! THIS IS WHY WE TOOK IT FROM C.S.U. AT THE SCENE IN THE FIRST PLACE!
HELLO?
HEY? HEY? MIJO? THIS IS PAPA.
YES?
I'M--I'M IN REAL TROUBLE, JUNIOR, A-A-AND SO--I NEED, *UH*--YOU TO TURN YOURSELF IN, *NIÑO.*
YOU LISTENING, ASSHOLE? YOU HEAR ME? EVERY MEMBER OF YOUR FAMILY IS GONNA DIE.
I DON'T CARE WHAT THIRD-WORLD SHITBOX THEY HIDE IN. WE'RE GONNA FIND THEM.
YOU FUCKED UP, AND YOU FUCKED UP GOOD, AND IF YOU DON'T COME IN AND TAKE YOUR MEDICINE FOR IT, DADDY'S DEAD.
MOMMY'S DEAD. LITTLE SISTER'S DEAD.

YOUR DOG, YOUR CAT, YOUR THIRD-GRADE TEACHER, YOUR MAILMAN, THAT JOGGER WHOSE SPANDEX ASS YOU OGLED ON THE SIDEWALK, THEY ARE ALL FUCKING DEAD!
AM I GETTING THROUGH TO YOU, YOU BABY-KILLING PIECE OF SHIT?!
AAAAAH-- AH GOD! THEY'RE ANIMALS! THEY'RE FUCKING ANIMALS--
HELP ME, JUNIOR! HELP YOUR DADDY!
I UNDERSTAND.
GREENE! ¿QUÉ PASA?
WELL?
DEATH THREAT. FRIEND OF THE VICTIM'S. DIDN'T LEAVE A NAME.
DEATH THREAT? THAT WAS MORE LIKE A DEATH NOVEL. GEEZ...
NOW HELP ME LOOK FOR CLUES. YOU KNOW, LIKE IN THE MOVIES?

I GOT THE LOWDOWN ON YOUR POOL VIC.

SHOOT.

THERE IS NO CONTUSION, NO LACERATION, NO ABRASION, NO PUNCTURE WOUND, NO SLASH WOUND ANYWHERE ON THIS ENTIRE...

...WELL, CALLING IT A **"BODY"** WOULD BE GENEROUS. THIS CONTIGUOUS AMALGAMATION OF SKIN AND HAIR. NOT A MARK ON IT.

JUST NO BONES, NO CARTILAGE, NO ORGANS, NO BLOOD VESSELS, NO EYEBALLS.

IN OTHER WORDS...

...GREENE WAS ***RIGHT.*** WHAT ELSE IS NEW LATELY?

WHY DO PEOPLE KEEP SAYING THAT LIKE IT'S AN EXPLANATION?
MISSING PERSONS IS WORKING ON AN I.D. BUT DON'T HOLD YOUR BREATH.
WHY, WHAT'S THE PROBLEM?
HOW TO PUT THIS...WELL, TRIVIA, YOU KNOW MICHAEL MYERS FROM HALLOWEEN?
CREEPY CHALK-WHITE MASK SLASHER DUDE?
IN THE ORIGINAL MOVIE, THAT CHALK-WHITE MASK WAS ACTUALLY A WILLIAM SHATNER CAPTAIN KIRK MASK TURNED INSIDE OUT.
SO WHAT WE GOT HERE ON THE SLAB IS MICHAEL MYERS...
...WHICH WE GOT TO SOMEHOW MATCH TO WILLIAM SHATNER. YOU DIG?
GEE, THAT'S A REALLY HELPFUL ANALOGY, HARRIS, THANKS.
I LIVE TO SERVE.
VIC WAS WEARING A PAIR OF THOSE SPANDEX BIKE SHORTS IN THE POOL.
MAYBE IF YOU NARROW IT DOWN TO PEOPLE WHO DISAPPEARED WITH BIKES OR HAD BIKING AS A HOBBY.
GOOD CATCH, SANA. ON IT.

GOTTA MOTOR. I AM ABOUT TO GET TORN A NEW ASSHOLE WITHOUT ANESTHETIC.
Wife
Answer
LAY BACK AND THINK OF ENGLAND.
HEY, BEV, WHAT'S--
YOU DON'T KNOW IF YOU'RE COMING HOME FOR DINNER?
THIS IS WORSE THAN YOU BEING UNDERCOVER--AT LEAST THEN YOU WERE PREDICTABLY IGNORING ME!
I AM NOT IGNORING YOU. I'M ON A STAKEOUT.
AT A STRIP CLUB?
I WISH!
UH...I MEAN OF COURSE NOT, MY BELOVED WIFE...
NICE SAVE.
I HAVE DONE NOTHING BUT, AND I AM NOT MAKING THIS UP, WATCH A GUY STARE AT HIS CAT SINCE THE MINUTE HE GOT HOME.
I SHALL DO IT. THAT IS AN EXCELLENT PLAN.
OF COURSE IT IS. I CAME UP WITH IT.
I'D THINK HE WAS TALKING TO IT BUT I HAVEN'T SEEN HIS LIPS MOVE.
I ALMOST WANT TO KILL MYSELF IN SYMPATHY.
SO BORED

OH, FINALLY, PRAISE JESUS, HE'S GOING SOMEWHERE. MAYBE IF I'M LUCKY HE'LL DROWN HIMSELF...
...GOD, WHAT IS WITH THAT HAT?
GOTTA GO, HON. LOVE TO YOU AND THE SPUD...
UH-HUH.
RIGHT BACK AT YOU.

No this
isn't creepy

The Great Race has inhabited countless sentient worlds across the cosmos, and each time the pattern is the same.
You see the first signs at the margins of your society, among the invisible and the ignored.
They do not have the distractions to ignore what's right above your head the whole time.
FREAKY BLAIR WITCH SHIT WTF

The stars are right.
Things that could not live for millennia past now rise up from the depths of the seas and the stars.
Will need TETANUS SHOT
Where the hell did he GO?
They destroyed a people greater than your kind can literally imagine.

And now--it is happening again--it is happening to you.
But I will **change history.**

I will learn how to
defeat these creatures,
and bring the knowledge
back to save my people.

ANZIOS SAY-- FIND THE HOMELESS CAMP ON LOOKOUT HILL IN PROSPECT PARK, IN THE WOODS! GO THERE! ALONE! ELEVEN THIRTY! OR I'M A DEAD MAN!
I UNDERSTAND.
And I am sorry, Sana Fayez.
But I cannot let you **stop** me.

9'0"
8'0"
7'0"
6'0"
5'0"
4'0"

DON'T MOVE, SHITHEAD!
HYAA!
GAK!
HE SAID DON'T MOVE, OR THIS IS GONNA GO WAY WORSE FOR--
NGG!

I appear to have underestimated Detective Fayez.
She is...
WE WERE SUPPOSED TO BRING YOU IN ONE PIECE, BUT--
KRAKK
...unexpectedly **skilled.**
N.Y.P.D.! THAT'S ENOUGH!

JOIN THE FUCKING CLUB.
DETECTIVE FAYEZ, MINOR CRIMES.
MY PARTNERS AND I ARE WITH VICE.
HELL ARE YOU DOING?
HELL... HELL ARE YOU DOING?
Jesus these guys didn't get hit with the ugly STICK
I'M TAILING A SUSPECT.
OR I WAS, UNTIL YOU NUMBNUTS SCARED HIM OFF. HELL ARE YOU DOING?
YOU WORK FOR--
WE GOT A REPORT. HOMELESS EXPOSED HIMSELF OVER ON THE PLAY-GROUND BY THE BAND SHELL. WITNESS SAW HIM HEADING THIS WAY.
They got run over by the whole damn ugly TRUCK
SO YOU THOUGHT YOU'D ROUND UP A POSSE AND GET YOUR BRUTALITY ON, HUH?
I SHOULD REPORT YOUR DUMB ASSES RIGHT NOW.

YOU'RE JUST LUCKY I GOT MY OWN PROBLEMS.
SORRY ABOUT THE SCREWUP, DETECTIVE. YOU SURPRISED US, SNEAKING UP ALL NINJA AND SHIT.
WHATEVER. LEMME SEE IF THERE'S JUST A SLIM CHANCE MY GUY ISN'T IN THE WIND... SHIT!
COINCIDENCE?
HELL IF I KNOW.
I DO KNOW DAD'S GONNA BE PISSED.
FUCK HIM. OUR MOM'S GONNA BE PISSED.
JUST LUCKY I REMEMBERED I GOT THAT PHONY BADGE.
MAYBE THE LITTLE FUCKER'S AROUND HERE SOMEWHERE. YOU CHECK THAT WAY. I'LL GO THIS WAY.
GOT IT. MEET BACK HERE IN TEN.

Prubika is the sense of mind reading.
The same way a blind man reads Braille.
Hmh. Edgardo Sr. is being kept hostage on an Anzio barge in the harbor...

The question now is...
...how can I put this information to any use?
DREAMS IN DARKNESS
J.R. CARTER
DREAMS OF DEATH
J.R. CARTER

DAILY NEWS
NYDailyNews.com
"JUICE BOX" KILLER
NYPD Covers Up Skinning Psycho, Sources Say
CHIEF MALONE, PLEASE.
TELL HIM J. RANDALL CARTER IS CALLING.
SSSSSSSSS

HEY! HEY! DYLAN! WHAT Y'DOIN'?

GET OUT OF DERE! DAT'S FILT'Y AND DISGUSTIN'!

WHA'-- WHA' YOU FIND--

EEEEEEEEEE

EEEEEEEEEEEEEEEEEEEE

I will have to contrive some reason for Fayez and me to search the barge without a warrant…
MINOR CRIMES DIVISION
A judge would ask too many questions about where I got the lead from…

WHERE DID ALL THESE PEOPLE COME FROM?

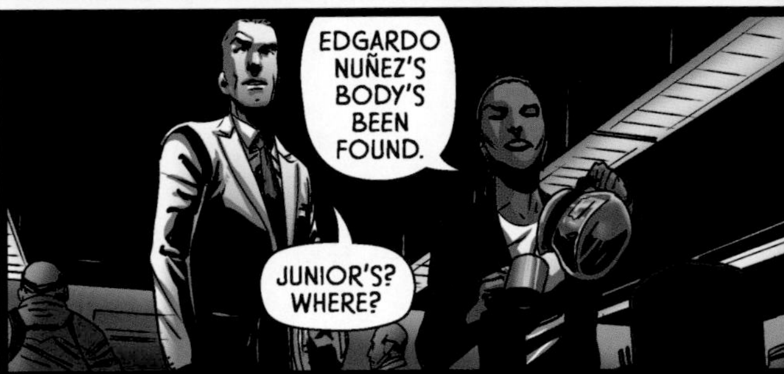
EDGARDO NUÑEZ'S BODY'S BEEN FOUND.
JUNIOR'S? WHERE?

PLAYGROUND, COBBLE HILL. OR HIS *SKIN* HAS, ANYWAY, JUST LIKE OUR SWIMMING POOL VICTIM-- WHO IS SPLASHED ALL OVER THE TABLOIDS THIS MORNING.
ALSO SOME POLICE BEAT REPORTER WITH TOO MUCH TIME ON HER HANDS DID SOME DIGGING AND FOUND WHAT LOOKS LIKE THE FIRST VICTIM.
SO CHIEF MALONE HAS CREATED A TASK FORCE WITH MAJOR CRIMES TO COMBINE ALL THREE INVESTIGATIONS INTO ONE.

CONGRATULATIONS, GREENIE BABY!
YOU GOT MORE PARTNERS THAN YOU COULD POSSIBLY ASK FOR!
TAP
TAP

SO WHAT'D YOU GET UP TO LAST NIGHT?
ME? NOTHING.
TOOK A WALK, WENT TO BED.
YOU?
ME?
I HAVE A EETHING BABY. I DID THE SAME THING I DO EVERY NIGHT.
NOT SLEEP AND CONTEMPLATE THE MERCIFUL EMBRACE OF DEATH.
Now that Edgardo Jr.'s body has been found, Anzio won't need to keep Senior around to use as a chip against his son…
His lifespan may be measured in hours, not days…

…unless someone recovers him…
A, UH, C.I. POINTED ME TO ONE POSSIBLE AVENUE OF INVESTIGATION, CAPTAIN. A BARGE, IN THE HARBOR?
THE KIND, UH, USED IN THE ANNUAL NATIONALIST CELEBRATION IN JULY-- THE KIND OF VESSEL THE PYROTECHNICS ARE FIRED FROM?
WHO'S YOUR "INFORMANT," GREENE? IS YOUR "INFORMANT" LICKING SOMEBODY'S BRAIN?
AND WHY DO YOU USE SUCH UNUSUAL PHRASEOLOGY?
That's how it always starts.
One mote, one flaw, abrading against the all-seeing eye of shared consciousness.
ANOMALY
ANOMALY DETECTED IN THE COLLECTIVE
And once the intruder was discovered, his fate…was…
PROBE HIM!
DON'T LET THE ALIEN GET AWAY!
HOLD HIM!
…sealed…

GREENE?
WH-- WHAT?

YOU GOT SOMETHING TO SAY?

NO. NO, SIR.

YOU AND FAYEZ ARE STILL PRIMARIES FOR THE PURPOSES OF PAPERWORK, REPORTING TO CAPTAIN LEONG, BUT NOW YOU'RE EQUAL MEMBERS OF A TEAM.
PUT US IN, COACH. WE'RE READY TO PLAY.

First alleged victim was a vagrant. His skin washed up in Brooklyn Bridge Park, by the water.

Like the sport cyclist, he was highly **mobile**-- either could have been taken **anywhere** in the city.
There's still some commonality we're missing…

"John Doe"
"Jane Doe"
Edgardo Nuñez

DETECTIVE FAYEZ.
A WORD, IF YOU PLEASE?

YOU HAD ONE JOB, SANA.
ONE JOB!
YEAH, I KNOW THAT MEME TOO, CHIEF MALONE, SIR.
AS I HAVE NOT HEARD ONE PEEP OUTTA YOU SINCE I ASSIGNED THIS INVESTIGATION--
IT'S BEEN A WEEK!
--I ASSUME YOU HAVE NOTHING TO REPORT?
OTHER THAN HE TALKS TO HIS CAT?
I DON'T NEED THIS, FAYEZ. I REALLY DON'T!
AND I NEED THIS "JUICE BOX KILLER" CRAP EVEN LESS--
DAILY NEWS
"JUICE BOX" KILLER
"ONE FEMALE DETECTIVE AT THE SCENE SAID, 'IT'S LIKE WHEN MY LITTLE NIECE EMPTIES A JUICE BOX.
"'SHE SUCKS IT DRY, UNTIL IT IMPLODES.'"
I-- I SAID THAT--BUT NOT TO THE PRESS--
BECAUSE YOU'VE KIND OF GOT A REPUTATION.
IT WASN'T. ME.

NOW THE PRESS HAS A READY-FOR-HOLLYWOOD NICKNAME FOR THIS SERIAL! NOW IT'S A STORY. NOW IT'S A LEDE.
NOW THE MEDIA'S GONNA GRAB A SPECULUM AND A FLASHLIGHT AND GO LIVE IN MY ASSHOLE UNTIL THIS NUTSACK'S CAUGHT!
MY SHITS GIVEN ABOUT YOUR CAREER WILL DWINDLE TO ZERO IF YOU DON'T GIVE ME SOMETHING I CAN MOVE AGAINST GREENE WITHIN-- LET'S CALL IT SEVENTY-TWO HOURS--
--OR IT'S YOUR DIRTY LAUNDRY THAT'S GOING TO BE AIRED IN PUBLIC. OKAY?
GOD FORBID GREENE MIGHT ACTUALLY BE ABLE TO HELP CATCH THE J.B.K....
THE PRIORITIES OF THIS DEPARTMENT ARE SO MESSED...
Dasein is the sense of becoming so in tune with your surroundings that you become indistinguishable from them.

UGH! YOUR COLLECTIVE CONSCIOUSNESS IS SO UTTERLY **USELESS...** YOU MIGHT AS WELL SMEAR FECES ON A WALL TO COMMUNICATE...
WHAT DO YOU MEAN **"YOU,"** TWO-LEGS?
YOU WON'T CATCH ANY SELF-RESPECTING **FELINE** HYPNOTIZED BY GLOWING SCREENS.
I CANNOT DISCERN WHAT "DIRTY LAUNDRY" MALONE HAS ON FAYEZ...
...AFTER I WAS ABLE TO DISCERN WHAT "DIRTY LAUNDRY" MEANS...
...I HAVE NO CHOICE BUT TO ATTEMPT A RESCUE OF EDGARDO SR. ON MY OWN...
CAN I ASK YOU A QUESTION? WHY DO YOU GIVE A CRAP ABOUT THIS GUY?
WHY STICK YOUR NECK OUT FOR HIM? HE HAVE SOMETHING TO DO WITH YOUR "MISSION" YOU KEEP GOING ON ABOUT?
NO...BUT HE IS CUT OFF FROM EVERYONE. ISOLATED.
ALONE.
I CAN **RELATE.**
WHY DO YOU KEEP STARING OVER THERE?
WAITING.
A LUXURY I CAN NO LONGER AFFORD...

MY RAINA... MY BEAUTIFUL DARLING...
SHE WAS FREE OF THE ***TAINT,*** YOU KNOW?
MY ***BOYS...*** TO A MAN...ONCE THEY WERE OLD ENOUGH TO ***DRIVE,*** THEY SHOWED IT...
AND BEFORE THEY WERE OLD ENOUGH TO ***VOTE,*** THEY SWAM OUT TO JOIN THEIR MOTHER IN THE HELL GATE...
I ***KNEW*** THE DEAL. YOU KNOW, I KNEW.
THIS WAS THE PRICE I WOULD PAY FOR GETTING IN BED WITH THE ***INNSMOUTH CREW...*** MY WIFE'S PEOPLE...
THEY KNEW HOW TO SMUGGLE IN THE SHIT WITHOUT NOBODY KNOWING--
THE D.E.A., THE CARTELS, I MEAN, ***NOBODY--*** WE TOOK OVER THIS TOWN...
STILL...ALWAYS WANTED TO HAVE A CHILD BY MY SIDE...TAKE CARE OF ME IN MY OLD AGE...RAINA WAS IT...
NOW ***YOU*** KNOW WHAT THAT'S LIKE...TO HAVE THAT ***TAKEN AWAY...*** THEY FOUND YOUR BOY, ALL SUCKED DRY...
MY BOY... DIDN'T DO NOTHIN' TO YOUR GIRL, MAN... ***I*** DIDN'T DO NOTHIN' TO HER...
I KNOW. STILL.
SOMEBODY'S GOTTA ***PAY.*** SOMEBODY'S ***GONNA*** PAY.
DON'T REALLY MATTER WHO.

ANTONIO ANZIO.
BUSY HERE...
I AM DETECTIVE SEBASTIAN GREENE, MINOR CRIMES DIVISION, N.Y.P.D.
YOU ARE UNDER ARREST FOR THE KIDNAPPING OF EDGARDO NUÑEZ SR.
GREENE?
SEBASTIAN GREENE...?
DROP THE GUN. KICK IT OVER TO ME.
THEN GET DOWN ON THE GROUND. LACE YOUR FINGERS BEHIND YOUR HEAD.
YEAH. GREENE...YOU'RE ONE OF TOMMY MALONE'S CREW. RIGHT?
DON'T I PAY HIM GOOD MONEY TO TELL YOU TO GO FUCK YOURSELF?
CHIEF MALONE.
WHAT-- WHAT ABOUT HIM?

FIND A RECYCLING BIN FOR THIS, WILL YA? IT'S EMPTY.
AND RECYCLING'S GOOD FOR THE ENVIRONMENT.
I DO NOT--
JACK DANIEL'S Tennessee WHISKEY
KLAK
WHSSSH
HEY, HONEY!
WE GOT DINNER GUESTS!

No...
I know.
I deserve this.
I have
failed you.
My mission is the polyp.
I should have been trying
to find the polyp all along.
You are denying me your
love in response. Perfectly
reasonable. I understand.
Our kind cannot die...
...but separation
from the fullness
of our collective
consciousness is
a curse **worse**
than death.
Please.
Please. I'll
be good.
I'll obey.
I'll leave this
worthless human
right now.
I'll--

NOT SURE WHAT I THOUGHT WAS GOING TO HAPPEN.
BUT THAT WAS ANTICLIMACTIC.

HEY, KITTY, KITTY.
DON'T TELL DADDY GREENE I WAS HERE THE WHOLE TIME, *HUH?*
Prrrr
THAT WOULD REQUIRE ME ACTUALLY GIVING A SHIT.

PFFFF.
FREAK.

Date
YOUR NAME
Your Address
Your City, State, Zip Code
$
Pay to The Order of
Dollars
Authorized Signature
Memo
1234 - 567898765 - 4321234

DATE
$
DOLLARS
PAY TO the order of

HRM.

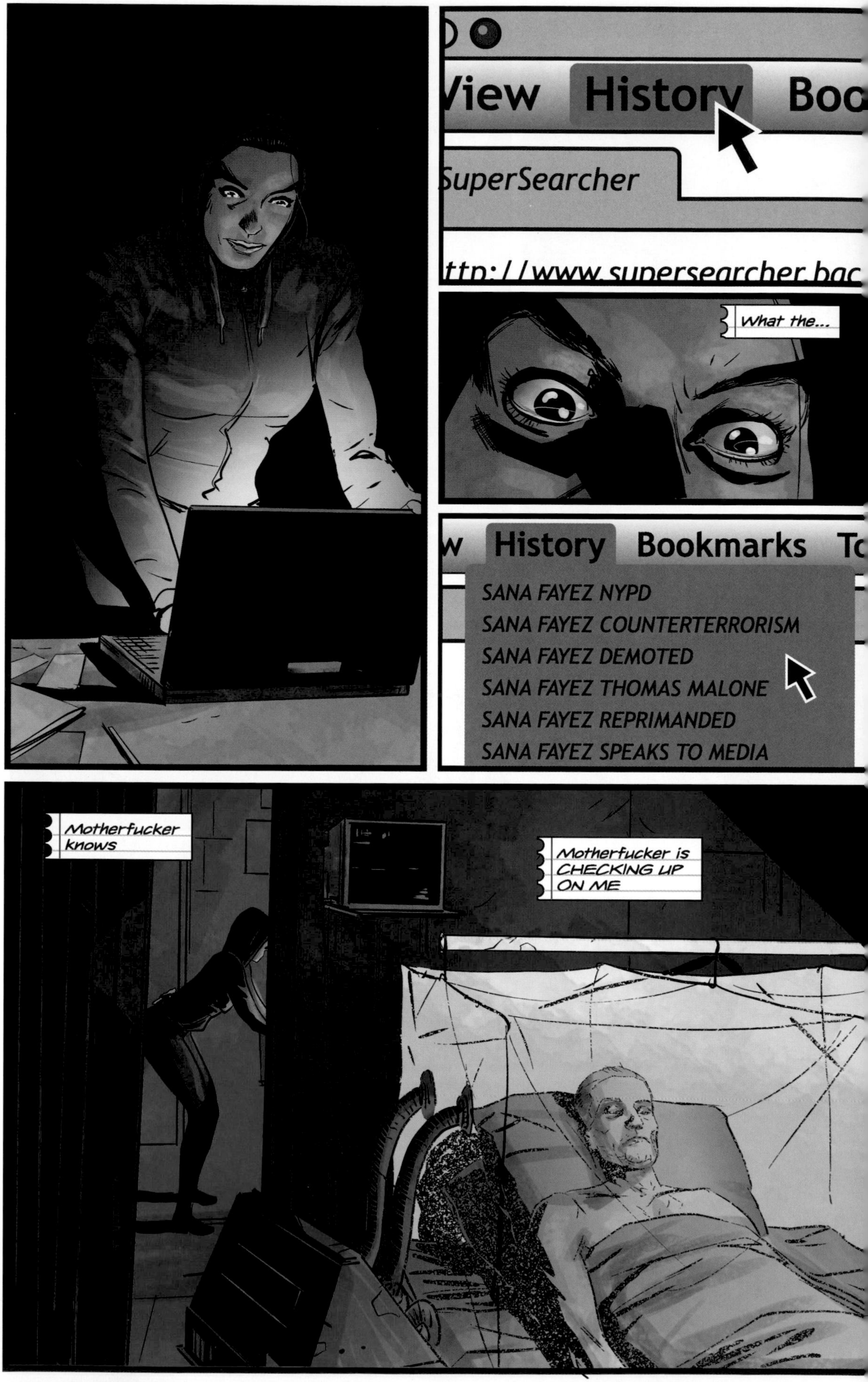

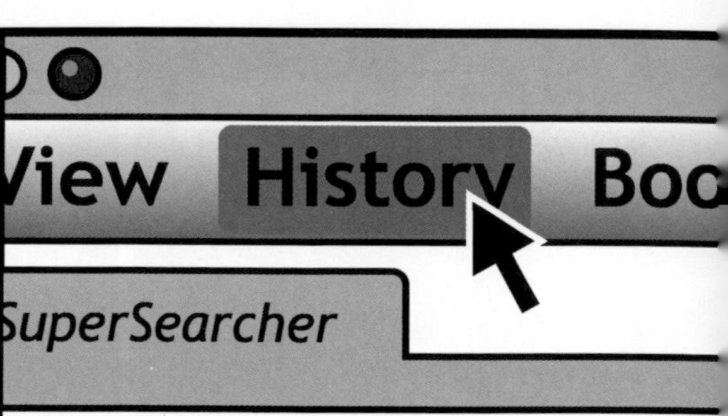

History Bookmarks

SANA FAYEZ NYPD
SANA FAYEZ COUNTERTERRORISM
SANA FAYEZ DEMOTED
SANA FAYEZ THOMAS MALONE
SANA FAYEZ REPRIMANDED
SANA FAYEZ SPEAKS TO MEDIA

Motherfucker knows

Motherfucker is CHECKING UP ON ME

WHAT'S GOIN' ON?
THAT'S WHAT I'M TRYIN' TO FIND OUT, YA PISSER!
WHAT THE...?
Fish-faced bros from the park last night
UNCA! UNCA ANZIO!
WHAT'S GOIN' ON?!
NOTHING TO GET YOUR PANTIES IN A BUNCH, BOYS.
JUST A PIGGY WHO FORGOT WHO FILLS HIS TROUGH.
YOUR AUNT'S TAKING CARE OF IT.

Join the police force, she said, serve your community
Girl what the hell were you even THINKING?!?!
Holy
COP'S PUTTING UP A WICKED FIGHT.
Is that Edgardo Nuñez Sr.?
I REMEMBER THIS GUY NOW...
GREENE.
MALONE USED HIM AS A BAG MAN, MOSTLY, DROPPING OFF, PICKING UP PAYMENTS...
WTF
HADN'T SEEN HIM IN A WHILE.
ASSUMED MALONE LOST FAITH IN HIM.
HEY, DON'T I KNOW YOU?

RELATED QUESTION:
FUCK YOU DOING HERE?

DROP IT!

BAM BAM

BAM BAM BAM
BAM BAM
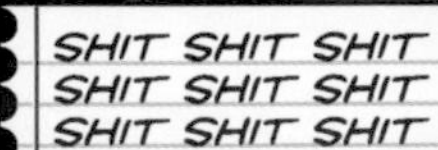
SHIT SHIT SHIT
SHIT SHIT SHIT
SHIT SHIT SHIT

...

DANGER: FIREWORKS
...shit?

SHOOT HIM!

I'M TRYING!

NO, YOU RED LOBSTER-SMELLING INBRED! SHOOT HIM! ***HIM!***

IT'LL LOOK LIKE HE CAUGHT ONE IN THE CROSSFIRE!

OH...

N.Y.P.D.!
HUH?
FWOOSAH
GYYAAHH!
HOLY CRAP!
EDGARDO! HOLD YOUR BREATH!
FWOOSH
PWEEE
FWOOOO

KRRAKK
POP
POP
BAM
POP
BOOM
CRACKLE
What just happened?

BOMF
PWEEEEEEEEE

NFFF...
NNHHH...
NNNOOO...
MALONE.
IT'S ME,
CARTER.
IT DIDN'T
SEEM POSSIBLE...
BUT SOMEHOW YOU
SCREWED IT ALL UP
WORSE THIS TIME,
MALONE.

I GIVE THIS SPEECH TO ALL THE DETECTIVES ASSIGNED TO MINOR CRIMES.
YOU MISSED IT ON YOUR FIRST DAY, FAYEZ, BECAUSE YOU GOT DUMPED IN MY LAP SO QUICKLY.
PETER LEONG JR., CAPTAIN
SO I AM GIVING IT TO YOU NOW.
WHEN I WAS FIRST ASSIGNED THIS DETAIL, I THOUGHT IT WAS BENEATH ME.
I THOUGHT THAT MY SKILLS WERE BEING UNDERVALUED. THAT I HAD KISSED THE WRONG BUTTS, GREASED THE WRONG PALMS.
THEN, AFTER I HAD DONE THE WORK FOR A WHILE, TAKEN THE CASES THAT DROP IN HERE AS IF FROM A SEWER, THE COLD CASES, THE IMPOSSIBLE WHODUNNITS...
...I REALIZED THAT THERE WAS A *LOT* OF GOOD WORK TO BE DONE HERE WITH THE SPOTLIGHT OFF YOU.
WHEN THE BOSSES AREN'T IN YOUR FACE TWENTY-FOUR-SEVEN, YOU CAN DO SOME REAL GOOD POLICE WORK.
BUT AFTER MANY YEARS OF DOING THAT, AND NO COMMENDATIONS COME YOUR WAY, NO PRESS, NO PAT ON THE BACK...
...I REALIZED, NO, I WAS RIGHT THE FIRST TIME. IT'S A ***"GO FUCK YOURSELF."***
SIR, I JUST DON'T UNDERSTAND. I SAVED AN INNOCENT MAN'S LIFE.
I BROUGHT DOWN AN ENTIRE WING OF THE ANZIO CRIME SYNDICATE.
AM I... AM I BEING ***DEMOTED?***

DETECTIVE FAYEZ, I AM NOT SURE WHERE YOU GOT THE IMPRESSION THAT THIS DEPARTMENT WAS A **MERITOCRACY,** BUT ALLOW ME TO DISABUSE YOU OF THAT NOTION IMMEDIATELY FOR YOUR AND MY OWN GOOD.
MINOR CRIMES IS A DUMPING GROUND FOR **LOSERS,** WHICH IS WHAT THE BRASS THINKS YOU TWO ARE.
WHEN YOU **SINGLE-HANDEDLY** DO THE WORK OF A **DOZEN** COPS IN ONE EVENING, THUS PROVING YOU ARE **NOT** A LOSER...
...AND WHEN YOU HUMILIATE THE CITY BY SHOWING THAT THE CONTRACTOR FOR THEIR ANNUAL JULY FOURTH FIREWORKS DISPLAY WAS HOPELESSLY **MOBBED UP...**
...YOU EXPECT TO BE **REWARDED** FOR YOUR INITIATIVE? OH, NO.
YOU WILL BE **PUNISHED** FOR **DARING** TO PROVE THE BOSSES **WRONG.**
I SEE HOW THAT AFFECTS DETECTIVE FAYEZ, SIR...
...BUT WHY DO **I** HAVE TO GO BACK TO WEARING THE UNIFORM TOO?
OFFICIALLY, DETECTIVE GREENE, **YOU** ARE BEING ASKED TO TEMPORARILY WORK IN UNIFORM TO AVOID VARIOUS OVERTIME RULES FOR PLAINCLOTHES ESTABLISHED IN THE LAST COLLECTIVE BARGAINING AGREEMENT.
BETWEEN YOU AND ME, THOUGH...
...I'D SAY YOU HAVE **ALSO** PISSED OFF THE WRONG PEOPLE.

YOU ARE TWO MISFIT TOYS MAROONED ON THE SAME PITIFUL ISLAND.
SIR... IS THERE ANYTHING YOU CAN SAY... ANYONE I CAN...
FOR CHRIST'S SAKE, FAYEZ.
YOU ARE LOOKING AT THE KING OF THE ISLE OF THE FUCKUPS.
OBVIOUSLY, I COULDN'T SAVE MYSELF, OR I WOULDN'T BE HERE.
WHAT THE HELL DO YOU THINK I CAN DO FOR YOU?
THE ONLY THING THAT KEEPS ME FROM EATING MY SERVICE REVOLVER...
...IS THAT CITY OF POOR BASTARDS WHO DEPEND ON US TO KEEP THEM FROM GETTING THEIR GUTS SCOOPED OUT BY A PSYCHOPATH.
WE HAVE AN I.D., FINALLY, ON OUR "JUICE BOX KILLER" VIC FROM THE POOL.
MISS SIERRA COHEN, FORMERLY OF RED HOOK, WHICH IS THE SAME NEIGHBORHOOD IN WHICH EDGARDO NUÑEZ JR. AND PRINCESS ANZIO MET THEIR ENDS.
Sierra Cohen
GO. CANVASS. THEY USED TO CALL US GUMSHOES FOR A REASON. START SUCKING UP TRIDENT OFF THE SIDEWALK WITH YOUR FEET.
AND IF YOU FIND ANYTHING OF INTEREST AT ALL, REMEMBER TO REPORT IT IMMEDIATELY TO MAJOR CRIMES SO THEY CAN GET ALL THE CREDIT.

NOK
NOK

HELLO, SIR.
"John Doe"

GOOD MORNING, MA'AM.
"MA'AM"? WHAT THE FUCK?

HOW OLD DO I LOOK TO YOU?
DON'T MIND HIM, MISS.
HE'S FROM CANADA.

DO YOU KNOW THIS WOMAN?
Sierra Cohen

HAVE YOU SEEN THIS MAN? HE'S HOMELESS.
IS HE DANGEROUS?
"John Doe"
NOT ANYMORE.

YOU MAY HAVE SEEN HER RIDING HER BICYCLE AROUND THE NEIGHBORHOOD.

IS THERE AN ADULT AT HOME?

OH, YES, YOU CAN PUT THE DELIVERY RIGHT OVER HERE.

MA'AM...?
I THOUGHT "MA'AM" WAS BAD.
HERE IT'S APPROPRIATE.
I hate this planet.
WE'RE NOT, *UH*...DELIVERY PEOPLE.
N.Y.P.D.? HENCE THE, YOU KNOW, THE BLUE AND THE BRASS?
OH, I'M SORRY, I WAS HOPING YOU WERE FROM THE BUTCHER SHOP.
WHEN MY WEEKLY ORDER IS LATE, IT PUTS A CRIMP IN MY WHOLE WEEK'S SUPPER SCHEDULE.
MMM. TRAGIC.
WOULD YOU MIND LOOKING AT SOME PHOTOS...?
SORRY I COULDN'T BE OF MORE HELP!
YEAH, THAT'S OKAY.
YOU AND EVERYONE ELSE IN YOUR DEAF-AND-BLIND HOOD...
HM. TOO BAD FOR THE OLD BAT.
WHY'S THAT?

Pork Shop

FOR RENT

STORE FOR RENT CALL (212) 555-5555

SHE'S GONNA BE WAITING A WHILE FOR THAT MEAT ORDER.

STORE FOR RENT CALL (212) 555-5555

OH GOD DAMN IT--
KRNCH

--FUCKING--

GOD DAMN IT! POUNDING THE BEAT AGAIN!
BEV IS NEVER GOING TO LET ME HEAR THE END OF IT!
WE NEED TO TALK.

YEAH. WE DO.
ENOUGH IGNORING THE 900-POUND GORILLA.
GORILLA? WHERE?!

YOU DUMB MOTHERFUCKER.
THE FACT YOU HAVEN'T EVEN ASKED ME ABOUT EDGARDO NUÑEZ SR. ALL MORNING MAKES YOU THE GUILTIEST SON OF A BITCH SINCE O.J.

I KNOW YOUR SECRET.
AND I'VE ALREADY TOLD THE F.B.I.

SORRY I COULDN'T BE OF MORE HELP!
A LADY POLICEMAN! AND AN A-RAB TOO, FROM THE LOOKS OF HER.
HOW ABOUT THAT.

SO STRONG AND CONFIDENT.
MAYBE IF THEY ALLOWED SUCH THINGS WHEN I WAS A GIRL...

BOUCHER'S WATER CARNIVAL

AH, WELL. C'EST LA VIE, ISN'T THAT RIGHT, TOBY?

AFTER ALL, IF MY LIFE HAD BEEN DIFFERENT...

...I MIGHT NEVER HAVE MET YOU...

POLICE

UNITED STATES
POSTAL SERVICE

DETECTIVE FAYEZ?
YES?
I'M SPECIAL AGENT O'DEA. THIS IS SPECIAL AGENT MANDELSON.
GOOD TO MEET YOU.
DID YOU GET THE CHANCE TO LOOK AT THE MATERIALS I SENT OVER?
WE HAVE. IT'S AN INTERESTING CASE...THOUGH A LITTLE LIGHT BY WAY OF EVIDENCE...
FBI
YEAH, UNFORTUNATELY WHEN THE ANZIO BARGE ***BLEW UP,*** MOST OF MY ***PROOF*** WENT WITH IT...
...EXCEPT WHAT I HAD SECURED IN WATERPROOF EVIDENCE BAGGIES BEFORE I LEFT GREENE'S HOUSEBOAT.
YES, WE LOOKED INTO YOUR DETECTIVE GREENE'S FILE...
...AND I CAN CERTAINLY SEE WHY CHIEF MALONE'S INTEREST WAS PIQUED. THE DETECTIVE'S CLEARANCE RATE ALMOST TRIPLED FOUR MONTHS AGO.
THAT PART I CAN'T REALLY EXPLAIN.
BUT IT SEEMS OBVIOUS TO ME NOW THAT CHIEF MALONE WANTED ME TO SPY ON GREENE MOSTLY BECAUSE HE WAS WORRIED GREENE STOPPED ***PLAYING BALL*** BY SELLING OUT THE DEPARTMENT TO THE ANZIOS AND OTHER MOBS.

WE'LL NEED CORROBORATING EVIDENCE TO SUPPORT THAT...
AND UNTIL WE GET SOMETHING WE CAN GO TO OUR U.S. ATTORNEY WITH, I'M AFRAID ANY ASSISTANCE WE COULD PROVIDE YOU WOULD BE MINIMAL...
AND-- SORRY TO INTERRUPT, CLARICE--I'VE GOT TO SAY--
THIS ISN'T THE *FIRST* TIME YOU BROUGHT SOMETHING TO THE BUREAU ON YOUR DEPARTMENT, DETECTIVE FAYEZ.
AND YOU CAN'T BLAME US FOR WORRYING YOUR... *STAYING POWER* WON'T BE ANY BETTER THAN LAST TIME.

NO, YOU'RE RIGHT. I LEFT YOU GUYS HIGH AND DRY LAST TIME.
BUT I'M THROUGH TRYING TO MAKE *PEACE* WITH THE N.Y.P.D.
BURN ME ONCE, SHAME ON YOU. BURN ME *TWICE, ET CETERA...*
SO YOU'RE TRYING TO BURN THEM BEFORE THEY BURN YOU, *HUH?*
JUST TRYING TO FREE UP THE JOBS OF THE PEOPLE WHO WON'T LET ME DO MINE.
RIGHT. WELL...
THOSE CHECKS YOU GOT FROM GREENE'S HOUSEBOAT?
THE ONES WITH TWO RADICALLY DIFFERENT SIGNATURES?
OUR HANDWRITING EXPERTS MAY HAVE DISCOVERED THE SECRET TO WHY YOUR PARTNER HAS BEEN ACTING SO STRANGELY...
SEBASTIAN GREEN
HELLO, SIR?
I JUST HAD A MEETING WITH ONE OF THOMAS MALONE'S N.Y.P.D. DETECTIVES?
A MISS...SANA FAYEZ?

I THINK YOU'LL WANT TO **HEAR** ABOUT IT...
REALLY?
DO GO ON, CLARICE.

HERE'S THE BAD NEWS FOR YOU, GREENE...
BRASS ALREADY HAS ALL THE DIRT THEY'RE EVER GONNA GET ON ME.
BUT YOUR SECRET... I DON'T THINK THEY KNOW THAT.
YET.
DO THEY?
AND...WHAT IS IT THAT YOU THINK YOU KNOW?
I KNOW YOU'RE DIRTY. I KNOW MALONE'S DIRTY.
YOU TURNED ON HIM FOR SOME REASON--WEEKLY ENVELOPE'S NOT FAT ENOUGH FOR YOU?
AND HE SICCED ME ON YOU.
EXCEPT--I'M NOT HIS ROBOT HE CAN PROGRAM WITH PROMISES OF A PENSION.
I'M PRETTY SURE I FOUND OUT WHAT MALONE WANTS TO KNOW ABOUT YOU.
AND IT'S NOT GONNA BE GOOD FOR YOUR FUTURE.
BUT I'M NOT GOING TO TELL HIM UNLESS I ABSOLUTELY HAVE TO.
YOU WANNA KNOW WHY?

BECAUSE YOU'RE MY **PARTNER.** WE'RE SUPPOSED TO LOOK **OUT** FOR EACH OTHER.
AND AS CORNY AS THAT SOUNDS, THAT STILL **MEANS** SOMETHING TO ME.
MAYBE THE **ONLY** THING.
WHEN A MAN'S PARTNER IS KILLED, HE'S SUPPOSED TO DO SOMETHING ABOUT IT. IT DOESN'T MAKE ANY DIFFERENCE WHAT YOU THOUGHT OF HIM.
HE WAS YOUR PARTNER AND YOU'RE SUPPOSED TO DO SOMETHING ABOUT IT. AND IT HAPPENS WE'RE IN THE DETECTIVE BUSINESS.
SO. YOU HELP ME NAIL **MALONE,** MY LIPS ARE SEALED ABOUT YOUR LITTLE ISSUES.
AND YOU **WILL** HELP ME WITH EVERYTHING YOU KNOW **IF** YOU WANT MY SILENCE.
BUT...
NO! NO BUTS! NO NEGOTIATION!
THIS IS THE DEAL IF YOU DON'T WANT TO WIND UP IN THE CELL NEXT TO HIM.
I'M NOT GONNA LET YOU AND MALONE GET AWAY WITH YOUR DIRT.
BECAUSE IF HE DOES, THERE'S NO REASON I WAS PUT ON THIS EARTH. THERE'S NO REASON I BECAME A COP.
THE BOSSES DON'T GET TO WIN. NOT ALL THE TIME.
AND DEFINITELY NOT **THIS** TIME.

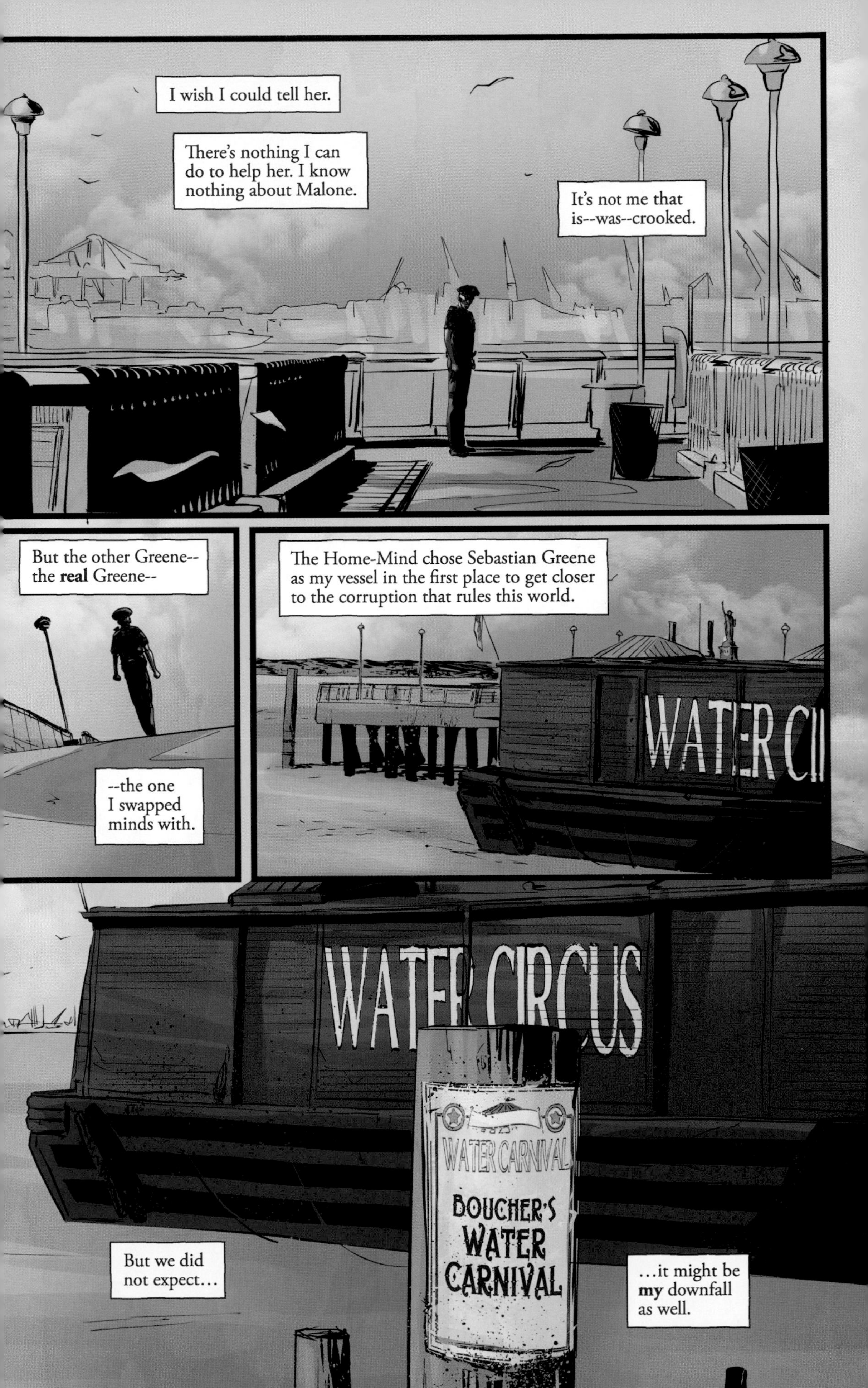

I wish I could tell her.
There's nothing I can do to help her. I know nothing about Malone.
It's not me that is--was--crooked.
But the other Greene--the **real** Greene--
--the one I swapped minds with.
The Home-Mind chose Sebastian Greene as my vessel in the first place to get closer to the corruption that rules this world.
WATER CI
WATER CIRCUS
WATER CARNIVAL
BOUCHER'S WATER CARNIVAL
But we did not expect…
…it might be **my** downfall as well.

I STOPPED BY EARLIER, MRS. BOUCHER?
I AM A MANHUNTER WITH THE MUNICIPAL WATCHMEN.
OH, OF COURSE, OF COURSE. I REMEMBER YOU. COME IN!

YOUR A-RAB PARTNER ISN'T WITH YOU?
NOT AT PRESENT, NO.
TEA?

DEAD LEAVES BOILED IN WATER?
NO, THANK YOU. I DON'T REALLY SEE THE APPEAL.

I DON'T GET TOO MANY VISITORS, YOU KNOW, NOT SINCE THE WATER CARNIVAL CLOSED DOWN.
WATER CARNIVAL?

OH, YES, IT WAS WONDERFUL. IT WAS EMIL'S IDEA-- HE WAS *MISTER* BOUCHER.
HE FOUND ALL THESE AMAZING ACTS--A FLEA CIRCUS-- A SEAMAN WITH NO ARMS WHO COULD PLAY THE FIDDLE WITH HIS FEET--
BOUCHER'S WATER CARNIV
--AND WE WOULD TOUR ALL AROUND THE DIFFERENT WATERFRONT COMMUNITIES IN THE TRI-STATE AREA ON OUR BARGE.
HOW THEY WOULD COME RUNNING. IT WAS QUITE A SIGHT TO SEE.
WHAT HAPPENED?
DAMN IDIOT BOX. FIRST IT WAS A COUPLE HOMES, THEN TWENTY, THEN A HUNDRED--THEN EVERYBODY.
THEY JUST STOPPED COMING. ALL TRAPPED IN THEIR HOUSES BY ED GODDAMN SULLIVAN.
I WON'T HAVE ONE IN THIS HOUSE TO THIS DAY. TOBY COMPLAINS SOMETIMES, BUT I PUT MY FOOT DOWN.
AS LONG AS YOU'RE IN *MY* HOUSE, I SAY--

TOBY? WHO IS TOBY?
HE'S MY--
fweeeee
WELL, NOT MY SON, REALLY, BUT HE'S MY WARD.
HE'S ALL I'VE HAD SINCE EMIL DIED. HE WAS THE WATER CIRCUS'S STAR ATTRACTION.
"THE MERMAID BABY," YOU KNOW? WE KEPT HIM IN A BIG JAR, AND--
OH, OFFICER.
OFFICER! I'VE GOT YOUR TEA!
I BELIEVE I TOLD YOU I DID NOT WANT ANY TEA.
YOU CAN'T GO BACK THERE, SIR!
TOBY--
HE DOESN'T LIKE STRANGERS--

SSPPSSSSHH
MA'AM.
I AM AFRAID YOU DO NOT POSSESS THE TECHNOLOGY REQUIRED TO SIGNIFICANTLY DAMAGE THIS BODY.
APOLOGIES.
NNNGGGK!
BUT I IMAGINE, WITH REGARDS TO TOBY-- YOUR HUSBAND CAUGHT HIM IN THE OCEAN SOMEHOW?
ONE OF-- KKK--ONE OF THE RED HOOK FISHERMEN DID--
WELL, HE WAS IMPRISONED BY MY PEOPLE MANY MILLIONS OF YEARS AGO AT THE BOTTOM OF THE SEA.
THE GREAT RACE DESIGNED THE POLYPS TO BE OUR SLAVES. BUT WE OVERREACHED. WE GAVE THEM TOO MUCH AUTONOMY.
THEY REBELLED AGAINST US, AND WE HAD TO PUT THEM DOWN.

WE THOUGHT WE HAD DEFEATED THEM FOREVER.
BUT WE WERE WRONG.
BOUCHER'S WATER
WHUD
THEY ALL BREAK FREE OF THEIR PRISON, MANY MILLIONS OF YEARS IN OUR FUTURE. JUST AS YOUR TOBY DID HERE IN THE PRESENT.
SO I HAVE BEEN SENT HERE TO FIND A WAY TO DESTROY THEM ONCE AND FOR ALL. BEFORE THEY DESTROY US.
I CAN USE THE SENSE OF ***RENNAKESH*** TO SEE YOUR MIND.
AGE AND DISEASE HAVE CLEARLY INTERFERED WITH ITS PROPER PROCESSES AND FUNCTIONS.

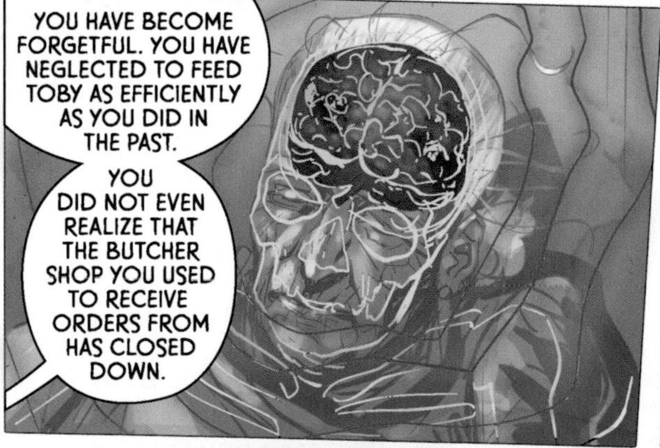
YOU HAVE BECOME FORGETFUL. YOU HAVE NEGLECTED TO FEED TOBY AS EFFICIENTLY AS YOU DID IN THE PAST.
YOU DID NOT EVEN REALIZE THAT THE BUTCHER SHOP YOU USED TO RECEIVE ORDERS FROM HAS CLOSED DOWN.

SO TOBY IS NOW GOING OUT AND GRABBING RANDOM PEOPLE OFF THE STREET.

ALREADY TWO MEN AND A WOMAN HAVE DIED THIS WAY.
I AM AFRAID I MUST PUT A STOP TO THIS.

NO! DON'T YOU DARE!
HE'S ALL I HAVE!
MY ONE AND ONLY!

Correction.
Three men and a woman.
UNITED STATES POSTAL SERVICE

BOUCHER'S WATER CARNIVAL
SKRASHH
He's under--
GLLRRGG
He's under the whole--
Didn't realize--he'd get so big so--

BOOM
WHAM
NGGUHH!
GAH!
SNAPP
Not prepared for a polyp this size.

Not prepared.
Stupid.
Sloppy and so very **stupid.**
This body is about to be catastrophically compromised.
Return to Home-Mind in disgrace.
No.
Wait.
No.
Use **ranos**.
Change vibrations-- escape through solid matter.

Hm.
Perhaps he wasn't prepared to confront one of his **masters,** either.
Toby knows he's a fugitive. His time in New York City, fat and happy, fed and hidden, has been like living a fantasy.
And I am reality, knocking on the door at last.
But now…
…I've got him right where I want him.

THERE ISN'T ANYTHING ABOUT YOU THAT ISN'T SUPER WEIRD.
YOU KNOW THAT, RIGHT?
I DO NOT KNOW THAT, NO.
NOK NOK
YES? HELLO?
ARE YOU SURE YOU HAVE THE RIGHT HOUSEBOAT?
YOU'RE-- SEBASTIAN GREENE? SANA FAYEZ'S PARTNER?
I HAVE THAT DISTINCTION, YES.
I'M HER WIFE, BEVERLY--

AH, YES. I RECOGNIZE YOUR OFFSPRING.
GOOD TO SEE YOU AGAIN.
HOW HAVE YOU BEEN?
GLLRRG?
I--I HAVEN'T SEEN SANA FOR 36 HOURS, AND SHE HASN'T CALLED ME, AND--AND IT'S JUST NOT LIKE HER.
I HAVE NOT SEEN HER IN THAT TIME EITHER, BUT WE HAVE BEEN OFF DUTY.
I DON'T-- SHE DOES NOT MAKE ME AWARE OF HER MOVEMENTS DURING NONWORKING HOURS.
OH? SHE SAID--SHE SAID YOU TWO ARE CLOSE.
SHE... DID?
SOMETIMES... I DON'T WANT TO BRING YOU INTO OUR PERSONAL BUSINESS, BUT...
...WELL, SOMETIMES SHE HASN'T BEEN...UH, THE MOST FAITHFUL... PARTNER IN THE WORLD...
UM...
I KNOW, I KNOW, OVERSHARING, PROBABLY, I KNOW. I'M SORRY TO DRAG YOU INTO THIS, BUT I HAVE THIS FEELING...
AND IF YOU WERE...COVERING FOR HER, FOR ANY REASON, I'M BEGGING YOU--
I CAN ASSURE YOU, MADAM, I HAVE NOTHING TO "COVER."
NOR ANYTHING TO COVER IT WITH...
IF YOU HEAR FROM HER, PLEASE... FOR ANY REASON... TELL HER...
...TELL HER I DON'T CARE WHY SHE'S GONE...I JUST WANT HER TO COME BACK. SAFE.

YOU LUCKY BASTARD.
WHAT?
SHE'S OUT OF YOUR HAIR. FOREVER.
I THINK WE SHOULD CELEBRATE. WITH CAT FOOD.
OR I WILL.
HONESTLY, I DON'T CARE WHAT YOU DO.
NO.
I THINK I'LL TRY TO SAVE HER.
I THINK I CAN.
WHAT? WE'VE SPENT ALL THIS TIME TRYING TO KILL HER! AND RIGHTLY SO!
AREN'T YOUR BOSSES GOING TO BE PISSED?
WHY WOULD YOU DO THAT?

BECAUSE.
THE HOME-MIND ISN'T HERE. IT HASN'T SEEN WHAT IT'S *LIKE* HERE.
THE *CUSTOMS* ARE DIFFERENT.
SHE'S MY *PARTNER.*
AND I HAPPEN TO BE IN THE *DETECTIVE* BUSINESS.

CRIME SCENE DO NOT CROSS

HIS NAME WAS ***MUSTAFA MAHMOUD.***

HE CAME ON OUR RADAR BY WAY OF CAIRO. EGYPTIAN MILITARY HAD BEEN SWEATING A TAJIK NATIONAL THE C.I.A. SNATCHED IN PRAGUE, RIGHT AFTER THAT DANCE CLUB BOMBING--IN SEOUL?

THIS TAJIK GUY, HE SWEARS ON HIS MOTHER'S LIFE, ON THE QURAN, WHATEVER THEY PUT IN FRONT OF HIM--THAT THEY'VE GOT A CELL RIGHT HERE, IN NEW YORK, RIGHT NOW, PLANNING TO BOMB NIGHTCLUBS IN MANHATTAN.

AND WE HAVE THIS THING CALLED ***FLEET WEEK*** COMING UP. ALL THE U.S. NAVY SAILORS EVERYWHERE, GETTING HAMMERED, LAID, AND HOPEFULLY NOT BLOWN UP.

NOW, THE NAME N.Y.P.D. GOT OUT OF CAIRO WAS MUSTAFA MAHMOUD, WHO TURNS OUT TO RUN A BAGEL KIOSK IN THE ***MEATPACKING DISTRICT...***

...WHERE ALL THE ***NIGHTCLUBS*** ARE.

OUR TEAM PICKS HIM UP AT HIS GARAGE IN ELEVENTH AVENUE JUST AS HE'S SUPPOSED TO HAUL HIS CART OUT FOR THE MORNING.

WE START SWEATING HIM ABOUT EIGHT, EIGHT THIRTY.

BY NOON HE STARTED ***CONFESSING*** TO STUFF. ANYTHING WE WANTED TO HEAR, BECAUSE HE THOUGHT, BECAUSE WE TOLD HIM, THAT WAS WHAT WOULD GET HIM OUT OF THERE.

BUT BY TEN HE'D RECANTED EVERY SINGLE THING. ALL THAT STUFF ABOUT HIM BEING INVOLVED IN THE NIGHTCLUB? ***THAT*** WAS THE LIE.

FLEET WEEK WAS STARTING IN ***TWENTY-FOUR HOURS,*** YOU KNOW?

TICK-TOCK.

TICK-TOCK.

AT ONE POINT, WE ORDERED OUT FROM THE DINER AROUND THE CORNER. ATE IN FRONT OF IT, JUST TO MESS WITH HIM.
A COUPLE OF US HAD SOUP, SO WE HAD THOSE, YOU KNOW, *SALTINE CRACKERS* WRAPPED UP IN THE *CELLOPHANE PACKETS?*
BELIEVE IT OR NOT, THIS IS ACTUALLY A TIME-HONORED *K.G.B.* TECHNIQUE.

"CRUNCH UP THE CRACKERS INTO CRUMBS. PUT THE CRUMBS IN THE PLASTIC BAG THE FOOD CAME IN.
"THEN TIE THE BAG OVER THE SUBJECT'S HEAD.
"THE SUBJECT INHALES THE CRUMBS. THEY CUT UP HIS LUNGS PRETTY GOOD.
"TORTURING A GUY WITH *CRACKERS?* CAN YOU *BELIEVE* THAT SHIT? ONLY THE *RUSSIANS.*
"AND *N.Y.P.D.*
"TURNS OUT THE GUY HAD A CONGENITAL LUNG CONDITION, THOUGH."

HE DIDN'T MAKE IT.

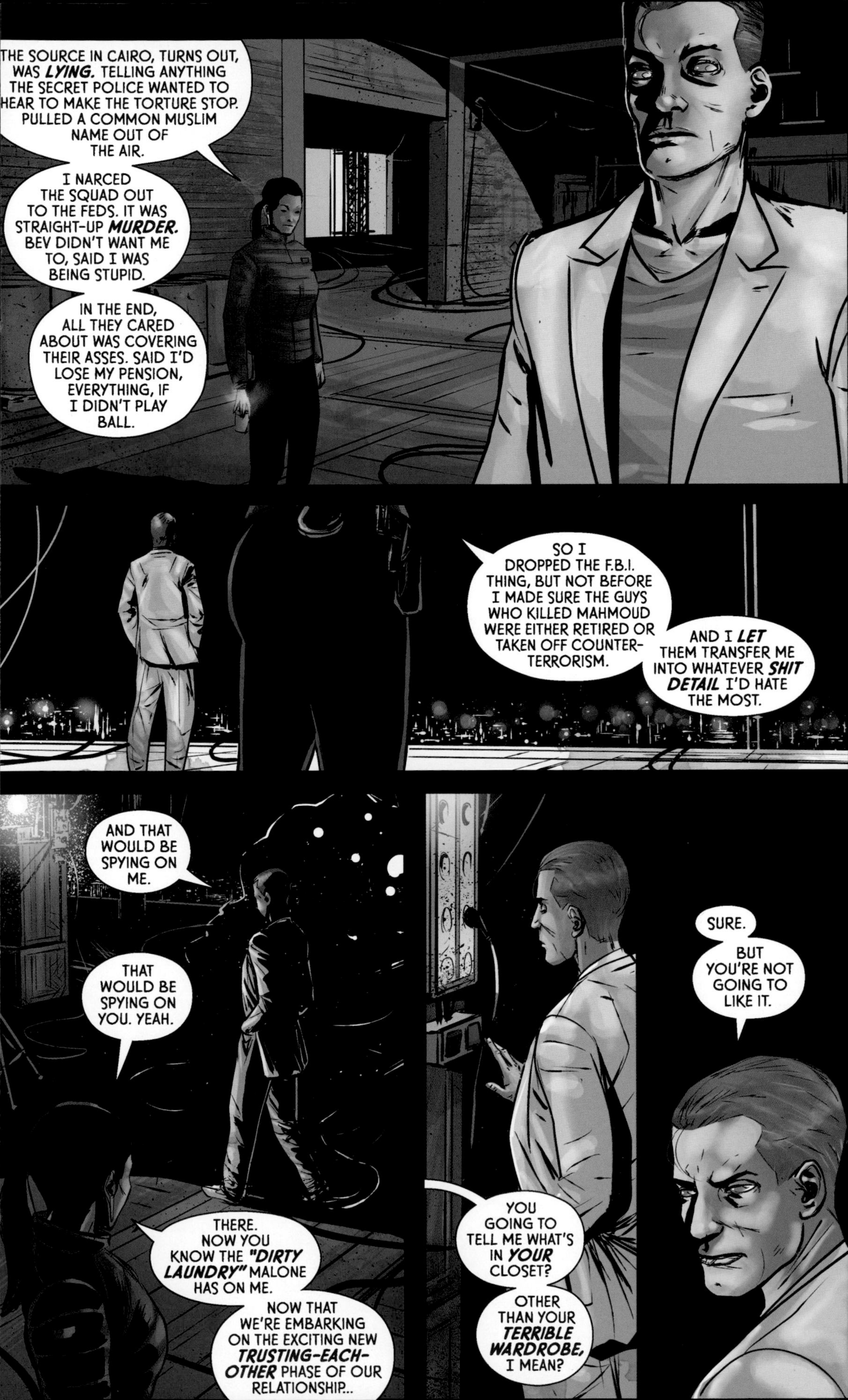

THE SOURCE IN CAIRO, TURNS OUT, WAS ***LYING.*** TELLING ANYTHING THE SECRET POLICE WANTED TO HEAR TO MAKE THE TORTURE STOP. PULLED A COMMON MUSLIM NAME OUT OF THE AIR.
I NARCED THE SQUAD OUT TO THE FEDS. IT WAS STRAIGHT-UP ***MURDER.*** BEV DIDN'T WANT ME TO, SAID I WAS BEING STUPID.
IN THE END, ALL THEY CARED ABOUT WAS COVERING THEIR ASSES. SAID I'D LOSE MY PENSION, EVERYTHING, IF I DIDN'T PLAY BALL.
SO I DROPPED THE F.B.I. THING, BUT NOT BEFORE I MADE SURE THE GUYS WHO KILLED MAHMOUD WERE EITHER RETIRED OR TAKEN OFF COUNTER-TERRORISM.
AND I ***LET*** THEM TRANSFER ME INTO WHATEVER ***SHIT DETAIL*** I'D HATE THE MOST.
AND THAT WOULD BE SPYING ON ME.
THAT WOULD BE SPYING ON YOU. YEAH.
THERE. NOW YOU KNOW THE ***"DIRTY LAUNDRY"*** MALONE HAS ON ME.
NOW THAT WE'RE EMBARKING ON THE EXCITING NEW ***TRUSTING-EACH-OTHER*** PHASE OF OUR RELATIONSHIP..
YOU GOING TO TELL ME WHAT'S IN ***YOUR*** CLOSET?
OTHER THAN YOUR ***TERRIBLE WARDROBE,*** I MEAN?
SURE.
BUT YOU'RE NOT GOING TO LIKE IT.

klik
KLAK
KLAK

KLAK
TUNK

NGGYYYY...
...YAAAAAHHH...
...GYAAHH!
NYUH YUH UHH YUHH

HELLO?
HERE.
I WASN'T SURE YOU'D COME.
I CONSUMED A PART OF YOUR BODY. AND THUS YOUR MEMORIES--YOUR THOUGHTS.
BUT YOUR FEELINGS TOWARD DETECTIVE FAYEZ WERE STRANGELY... **CONFLICTED.**
YOU THINK THIS IS A...NEGOTIATION OF SOME SORT?
YOU ARE ATTEMPTING TO BARGAIN WITH ME?
YOUR MASTER?

WE HAVE NO MASTERS BUT THE STARS.
YOURS IS A RACE OF COWARDS, FLITTING FROM ONE BODY TO THE NEXT ACROSS THE EONS.
YOU WERE FOOLS TO CREATE US...
...AND ALSO TO MAKE US YOUR BETTERS.
THAT REMAINS TO BE SEEN.
I REVEALED THE TRUTH ABOUT YOU TO HER.
I WAS GOING TO MAKE YOU LEAVE THIS WORLD, OR I WOULD TURN HER OVER TO YOUR SUPERIORS, WHO WOULD FIND AND DESTROY YOU.
BUT I HAVE CHANGED MY MIND.
YES?
I BELIEVE I WILL EAT HER INSTEAD.
AND DESTROY YOU MYSELF.
THEN TAKE YOUR PLACE.
I STOLE THE IDEA FROM YOU.
ISN'T THAT CLEVER?
YOU SHOULDN'T HAVE MADE US SO CLEVER.

WHAT WE *SHOULDN'T* HAVE DONE...
...IS MADE YOU ABLE TO *TALK.*
HEH.
HSSSSSS

THKRASH
KKLANG

IF IT MAKES YOU FEEL ANY BETTER, I WILL BE YOU BETTER THAN YOU COULD EVER BE.
I WAS BORN ON THIS PLANET. I HAVE OBSERVED THESE CREATURES AND THEIR WAYS FOR YEARS.
THIS IS JUST THE INEVITABLE.
IF I HADN'T DESTROYED YOU, THEY WOULD HAVE CAUGHT YOU SOON ENOUGH, ANYWAY.
WHAT DO YOU SAY TO THAT?
THAT WHILE YOU TOOK MY HAND...I AM IN YOU...AND THAT MAKES YOU IN ME.
TELLURITE IS THE SENSE OF KNOWING WHERE ALL PARTS OF YOUR BODY ARE AT ALL TIMES.
SO I KNEW WHERE YOUR LAIR WAS THE MINUTE YOU CHOSE IT. I'VE BEEN HERE FOR THE LAST HOUR AND A HALF.
PREPARING.

WH--
BLEEP
ENJOY YUGGOTH.
NNOOOOOOOO

SANA?
<I KNOW YOU ARE THERE, ALLAH. I KNOW YOU SEE MY TEARS.>

<I KNOW YOU HEAR MY PRAYERS. I KNOW YOU ARE TESTING ME.>
<I LOVE YOU, MY LORD. MY ALLAH. PLEASE KEEP ME SAFE. I KNOW YOU ARE THERE, ALLAH...>
SANA...?

NO!
NO!

STAY AWAY FROM ME!
YOU ARE A MONSTER!
A MONSTER!

YOU... YOU WANTED TO SEE ME, SIR?
YES AND NO.
I WAS HOPING YOU WOULD SEE ME.
TO TELL ME YOU HAD ONE OF YOUR DETECTIVES SPYING ON THE OTHER.
INSTEAD, I HAVE TO FIND OUT ABOUT IT FROM THE FEDS.
SIR...?
LYING SERVES ONLY TO ANNOY ME FURTHER.
GREENE...USED TO BE ONE OF OUR MOST TRUSTED MEN, SIR.
BAGMAN... LIQUIDATIONS... CLEANING...WHATEVER WE NEEDED.
THEN, OUT OF NOWHERE, SIX MONTHS AGO, HE HAD A TOTAL PERSONALITY CHANGE.
STOPPED TALKING TO ME. STOPPED RESPONDING TO MY ENCODED EMAILS.
I COULDN'T TRUST HIM ANYMORE, SIR. I NEEDED TO FIND OUT WHY.
THE F.B.I. FOUND OUT WHY. AND I WILL DECIDE WHETHER OR NOT TO ACT ON IT.

BUT YOU...I FIND I CAN NO LONGER TRUST *YOU.*
I CAN'T HAVE YOU GOING OFF ON ROGUE OPERATIONS INVOLVING THE *UNINITIATED.*

NOT UNTIL THE *STARS ARE RIGHT.*
AND *THE WISDOM* MAY OPERATE IN THE OPEN.

PERHAPS...IT *IS* BEST YOU KNOW, SIR. WE SHOULD CONTINUE TO INVESTIGATE GREENE. I...
LOOK, CALL IT AN OLD DETECTIVE'S *HUNCH,* MR. CARTER.
BUT HE'S *BAD* FOR US. FOR YOU.

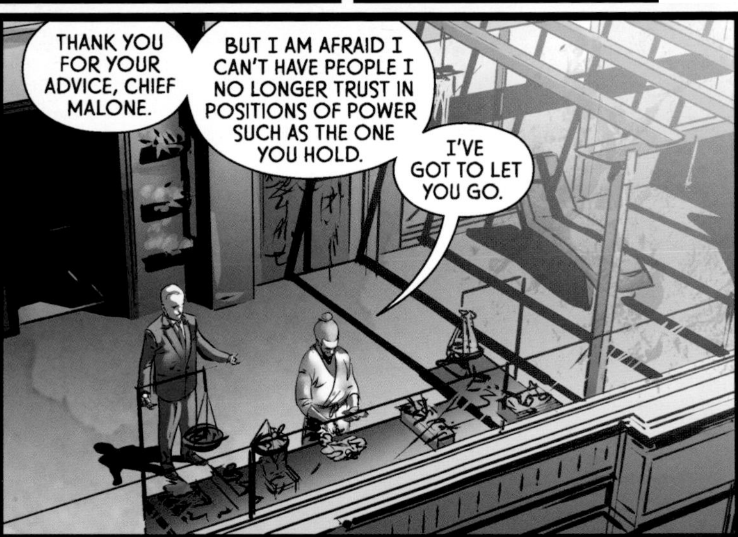
THANK YOU FOR YOUR ADVICE, CHIEF MALONE.
BUT I AM AFRAID I CAN'T HAVE PEOPLE I NO LONGER TRUST IN POSITIONS OF POWER SUCH AS THE ONE YOU HOLD.
I'VE GOT TO LET YOU GO.

I SEE.
I SUPPOSE THERE'S NO WAY I CAN TALK YOU OUT OF IT?
I'VE MADE UP MY MIND. I'M SORRY.

VERY WELL, THEN.
SHOULD I SEE MYSELF OUT?

NO.
THAT WON'T BE NECESSARY.
WH--

Happy Birth
WHO IS ONE? WHO IS ONE? WHO IS IT?

GO ON! BLOW OUT THE CANDLES! COME ON!
HE'S SCARED, SANA. MAYBE YOU SHOULD DO IT FOR HIM?

NO SON OF MINE IS GOING TO GROW UP SCARED OF FIRE! WHAT IF--
BWOOF

BEV, YOU'RE *BABYING* HIM.
GEE, I WONDER WHY? ***HE'S A BABY!***
SOMEBODY HID SANA'S GUN, RIGHT?
ding-dong

GREETINGS, LESBIANS.
HEY, GREENE.

YOU'RE... ALREADY HERE?

YEAH, THE FACEBOOK INVITE SAID ***ONE?*** BUT IT'S FINE. DON'T WORRY ABOUT IT.
DO YOU WANT A BEER? I GOT ***MOLSON*** FOR YOU--

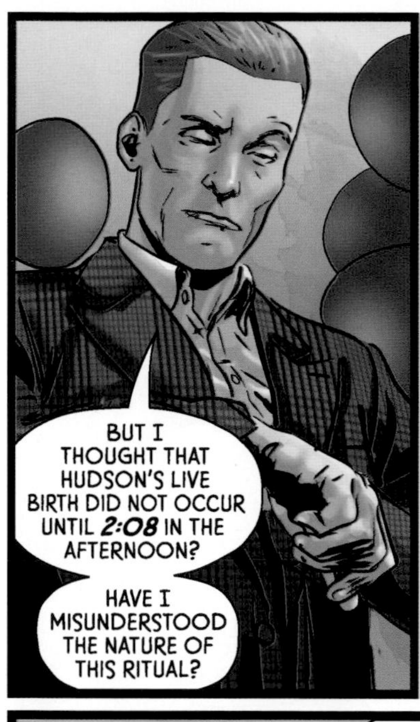
BUT I THOUGHT THAT HUDSON'S LIVE BIRTH DID NOT OCCUR UNTIL 2:08 IN THE AFTERNOON?
HAVE I MISUNDERSTOOD THE NATURE OF THIS RITUAL?

HOW...HOW DO YOU KNOW THE *EXACT TIME* I GAVE BIRTH?

I--

I DIDN'T?

HEY...WOW, IT'S...

...JUMPER CABLES...
I WAS INFORMED THAT IT IS BETTER TO... WHAT WAS THE PHRASING...?
"...BETTER TO HAVE IT AND NOT NEED IT THAN TO NEED IT AND NOT HAVE IT."

THANKS, SEBASTIAN, THAT'S VERY, *ER*...
...THOUGHTFUL?
WHO GIVES JUMPER CABLES TO A BABY--
HE'S CANADIAN.

MMMMM
HEY, "CHIEF." HOW'S THE NEW DIGS HOLDING UP?
FINE, EXCEPT THE STINK OF *MALONE* STILL LINGERS--
--PREPARATION H AND FAILURE.
BUT ENOUGH ABOUT ME.

HEY, GREENE! PUT YOUR GAME FACE ON!
WE CAUGHT ANOTHER ONE!
YOU ARE *SHITTING* ME.

THANK GOD FOR *MURDER.* THERE'S ONLY SO MUCH *DOMESTICITY* I CAN STAND BEFORE THE URGE TO STICK MY HEAD IN AN *OVEN* BECOMES OVERWHELMING.
I'LL DRIVE.
BUT--MY CAR IS ALREADY HERE--

I'LL BRING YOU BACK AFTER. SORRY, I DON'T WANT TO GET IN A CAR WITH YOU IN YOUR CONDITION.
MY...?
OH, COME ON, GREENE. MALONE HAS *VANISHED.* I'M NOT SPYING ON YOU ANYMORE. NO MORE BULLSHIT, OKAY?

I SWIPED TWO CHECKS FROM YOUR HOUSEBOAT--WITH *COMPLETELY DIFFERENT HANDWRITING.*
THE F.B.I. HANDWRITING LAB FIGURED OUT YOUR SECRET.

ONLY *ONE* EXPLANATION FOR THAT, THEY SAID.

YOU HAD A **STROKE.**
A... UH... A WHAT?

COME ON. IT'S RARE IN GUYS AS YOUNG AS YOU, BUT IT'S NOTHING TO BE ASHAMED OF.
WHAT WAS IT, LIKE, A BRAIN ANEURYSM OR A BLOOD CLOT? I DID SOME GOOGLING...
*UH...*IT WAS...IT WAS THE FIRST ONE YOU SAID.

YOU SLY DOG! YOU HID IT FROM THE DEPARTMENT BECAUSE YOU DIDN'T WANT TO BE FORCED ONTO ***DISABILITY*** BEFORE EARNING YOUR FULL ***PENSION.***
YES.
VERY SLY.

DON'T WORRY, YOUR SECRET'S SAFE WITH ME. PERSONALLY, I COULD CARE LESS. FROM WHAT ***I*** HEARD, YOU'RE ONE OF THE FEW PEOPLE WHOSE PERSONALITIES WERE ACTUALLY ***IMPROVED.***
"I'M FROM CANADA"...*HA!* THAT MIGHT PLAY WITH THE ***RUBES,*** BUT NOT A TRAINED ***MURDER POLICE*** SUCH AS MYSELF.

YES, YOU CAUGHT ME, SANA...*HEH-HEH...*YOU ARE A GOOD DETECTIVE.
NO SHIT, SHERLOCK!
I ALWAYS WANTED TO SAY THAT.

There are some, I imagine, who would **disapprove** that I manipulated Detective Fayez's mind for **selfish** reasons.

But I am so very far from home.

With no hope of returning soon.

I had built the fullness of other consciousnesses around me.

And no longer felt so alone.

PETER LEONG JR.
CHIEF OF DETECTIVES

And there are some mysteries...

...best left unsolved.

PINUP ARTWORK BY FRANCESCO FRANCAVILLA

PINUP ARTWORK BY RAFER ROBERTS

FROM *NEW YORK TIMES* BEST-SELLING AUTHOR

FRED VAN LENTE

industry. Every word from his pen reinvents what comics are capable of."
—Joshua Hale Fialkov
(*The Bunker; The Life After; I, Vampire*)

RESURRECTIONISTS

Art by Maurizio Rosenzweig and Moreno Dinisio

Jericho Way has discovered he's a Resurrectionist, one of a select group of people who can not only remember their past lives, but *become* them. Two groups are now after his services, and if Jericho joins them, he may steal back his own future!

ISBN 978-1-61655-760-7 | $19.99

CONAN AND THE PEOPLE OF THE BLACK CIRCLE

Art by Ariel Olivetti

After an agent of the dreaded Black Seers of Yimsha assassinates the king of Vendhya, his sister Yasmina—now a queen—vows revenge! But her plans are derailed when Conan kidnaps her, and soon the Cimmerian has ruthless mercenaries, vengeance-crazed tribesmen, sinister sorcerers, and an entire army hard on his heels!

ISBN 978-1-61655-459-0 | $19.99

THE COMPLETE SILENCERS

Art by Steve Ellis

In a city full of superpowered do-gooders, the mob needs above-average enforcers. Enter the Silencers, supercriminals who are happy to use lethal force for a mafia-funded payday. When the Silencers' leader finds out he's being set up for a deadly fall, these pawns do more than put a mob king in checkmate . . . They want to take over the whole city's crime scene.

ISBN 978-1-61655-540-5 | $19.99

ACTION PHILOSOPHERS

Art by Ryan Dunlavey

Study the tenets of Plato, the wrestling superstar from ancient Greece; learn the lessons of Nietzsche, the original *Übermensch*; and meditate on the messages of Bodhidharma, a kung fu master. Laugh, learn, and laugh some more, as Van Lente and Dunlavey deliver this comprehensive cartoon history from the pre-Socratics to Jacques Derrida!

ISBN 978-1-61655-539-9 | $29.99

FROM *NEW YORK TIMES* BEST-SELLING AUTHOR

FRED VAN LENTE

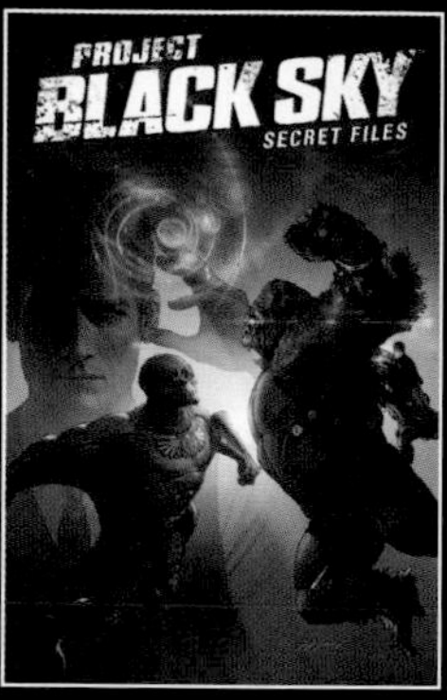

PROJECT BLACK SKY: SECRET FILES

Art by Michael Broussard, Steve Ellis, and Guiu Vilanova

In the late 1930s, a covert government agency was established to protect Earth from potential extraterrestrial threats. These brave men and women were called Project Black Sky, and what they discovered would change the course of human history.

ISBN 978-1-61655-604-4 | $14.99

BRAIN BOY VOLUME 1: PSY VS. PSY

Art by Freddie Williams II, R. B. Silva, and Rob Lean

When the United States Secret Service needs to stop an assassination before the killer's even decided to buy a gun, they call the world's most powerful telepath: Matt Price, a.k.a. Brain Boy. But when the secret agent that can read anyone's mind finds that a powerful psychic network has been hidden from him, Brain Boy begins to wonder whether he knows everything or nothing at all!

ISBN 978-1-61655-317-3 | $14.99

BRAIN BOY VOLUME 2: THE MEN FROM G.E.S.T.A.L.T.

Art by Freddie Williams II and Jeremy Colwell

Agent Price's new mission pits him against a doomsday-cult leader with a political agenda that poses a direct threat to the president. But a mysterious hive mind has more menacing plans for Brain Boy. He'll have no choice but to go head to head—brain to brain—with the mysterious Men from G.E.S.T.A.L.T.!

ISBN 978-1-61655-506-1 | $14.99

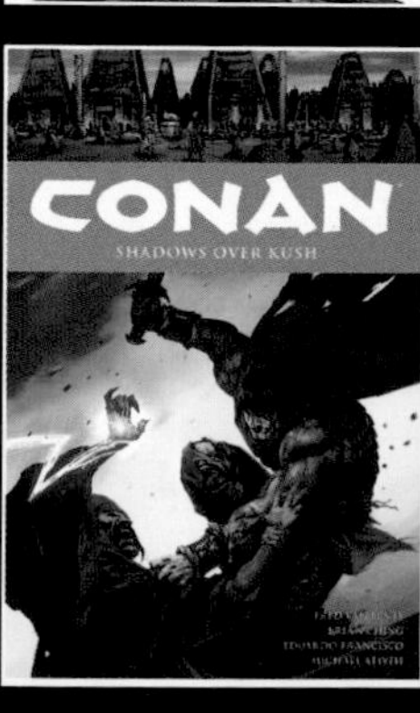

CONAN VOLUME 17: SHADOWS OVER KUSH

Art by Brian Ching and Eduardo Francisco

Conan drinks himself into a stupor while in the city of Shumballa—until an act of thievery propels him into a witch hunt full of adventure, demons, and rebellion! "By Crom! Now this is how a Conan story should read!" —Geeks of Doom

TPB: ISBN 978-1-61655-659-4 | $19.99
HC: ISBN 978-1-61655-522-1 | $24.99

AVAILABLE AT YOUR LOCAL COMICS SHOP OR BOOKSTORE! • To find a comics shop in your area, call 1-888-266-4226.
For more information or to order direct visit DarkHorse.com or call 1-800-862-0052 Mon.–Fri. 9 AM. to 5 PM. Pacific Time. Prices and availability subject to change without notice.